FORTUNE
—— AND ——
PARADISE

CLAY BRIDGES
PRESS

SHIRLEY MORGAN
Foreword by Jane M. Fortune

Fortune and Paradise
Copyright © 2022 by Shirley Morgan "The Star Lady"

Published by Clay Bridges in Houston, TX
www.claybridgespress.com

ISBN: 978-1-68488-012-6
eISBN: 978-1-68488-011-9

A Collection of Miracles
God has Performed in My Life

A miracle is anytime God answers prayer!
He is still in the miracle business 24/7!

It is the hope of the author that any chapter may
be used as a witnessing or educational tool,
as each one is complete on its own.

Contents

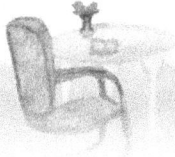

Foreword

Shirley wrote a book that shares how she exudes her faith in Jesus Christ. I first met Shirley while I was working as a Supervisor of a program for older adults while I was a younger adult. I remember meeting Shirley, the pleasant, attractive lady who would stand her ground. At this time, I did not understand how I needed Christ as much as I did during the second half of our relationship.

When I met her again, she was an Intake Assistant at a Christian counseling center and I had just begun there as a Resident Counselor. I found Shirley in the file room. I actually began the conversation by apologizing for "being hard" on her while she was in the program for adults. She told me in her firm, but kind way, "You were just telling me what I needed to do."

Then came my struggle. Both my siblings were struggling with cancer. My sister (being none too pleasant and afraid) was forty-six, had two children, a husband, and did not want to die. I was living in Virginia and had been going back and forth to Florida (to see her) and Texas (to see my brother) for several years. There was so much pain for me and my family.

Faithfully, as I would come into the Center and say hello to Shirley, she would ask about my sister and tell me, "I will pray for your sister." I went in to see Shirley one afternoon, as I often did before sessions. In her ever so pleasant manner, she again asked how my sister was feeling, as she had been praying for her. Having spoken on the phone with my sister earlier (I have become aware that we can "catch" anger from others), I realized she had "shared" her anger with me, so I was feeling the need to share. "Well, Shirley, I am not sure your praying is working - she is still so angry." I was frustrated, but silenced when Shirley firmly said, "Well, I haven't been saying the right prayer! I need to pray for her to open her heart to allow the Lord in." "Thank you, Shirley," I mumbled as I walked away.

I learned that her confidence was a "God confidence," and perhaps I needed to refine my communication with the Lord—especially when I am hurting and angry.

Thank you for sharing this book, Shirley. It is better than the lunch date we never had.

Jane M Fortune, LPC, LCMHC
www.carolinaforestcounseling.com
Licensed Professional Counselor
Licensed Clinical Mental Health Counselor

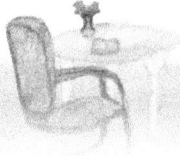

Preface

ortune is the last name of a woman God used to help me get a job and Paradis is the last name of a realtor God put in my life when I needed a home! GOD got me a job when I was jobless *and* a home when I was homeless! Keep reading! It is amazing!

The main thing I want everyone to know is that Father God is a loving Father who has answered countless prayers, urgent prayers: jobs, a home, healing from cancer, money! He has touched every area of my life. He has answered the secret prayers of my heart: the desire to be a missionary; the desire to use my artistic ability to touch others; and the desire to be a mother. Not only have I personally been blessed, but I have been blessed to be able to share God's Son, Jesus, with hundreds of people from all over the world who were visiting my hometown, Roanoke, Virginia. And, my paintings with God's Word on them, have gone with the people I met back to their hometowns all over the world! He has also graced me with my growing, beautiful, blessed family to the fourth generation. Every single question we have in life, He can answer. But we won't know that until we know Him, and know His voice, just like we know our best friend. Father God's love for us, His perfect love, is so much greater and deeper than we can ever understand, but I know without a doubt that:

God *knows*!
and is *interested* in! and wants to be *involved* in!
EVERY SINGLE part of our lives!

He did it for me, and He can do it for you!

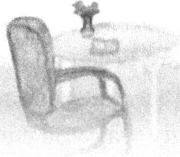

Introduction

My goal in writing my life story is the Salvation of Souls! *And,* for everyone to know how easy it is to know God! You can talk to Him as easily as you talk to your best friend . . . because He will respond!

It would be easier to go through life with all your sins hidden from public view; but really, that is impossible. There is always someone else who knows. So, as much as we can try to keep our past a secret, it can't be done. The biggest problem with bringing our past moral failures out into the open is not what other people think about us; it's what we, ourselves, think other people will think about us.

I know I'm very different now than I was when I deliberately lived in sin; but what I have learned is that a lot of people will define you by your mistakes in life, rather than by your good deeds, or even by the miraculous change Jesus Christ has made in who you really are. What I had to do was decide whose opinion was most important; and, of course, it has to be God's opinion or knowledge of who I have become—because He is the ultimate Judge. I also had to decide what my motive was for telling all. After a long life of seeking for meaning—which I firmly believe every person is doing—and now that I know what life is for, I want to share it, regardless of anyone else's negative opinion.

Every person ever born has to decide for themselves about God. God's Book, The Holy Bible, gives us an accurate description of Himself and mankind in Romans Chapter 1. Every person is a sinner and each one must decide for themselves whether or not they are going to believe God and accept His plan for freedom from the sinful state they live in—through Jesus Christ's death as payment for our sin—or deny Him and choose Hell. Every person born chooses one or the other. Heaven is where God lives, and you cannot go there unless you are perfect. God's plan is perfect because everything He does is perfect. God cannot allow wickedness into His perfect Heaven. The only way you can become perfect is to ask Jesus Christ to pay for your sins. That is why He died!

God knew that no person could willingly die to pay for his own sins; that death would send a person to Hell. Only a perfect person could die to pay for someone else's sins, and the only perfect person, of course, is God's own son, Jesus. The only way a person can use Jesus' death as payment for their personal sin is to ask Him to be their Savior.

YES! You can talk to Him. He is ALIVE! In Heaven, with God! And He does talk to people on this earth! God's plan is perfect, like everything He does is perfect. It wouldn't really be fair or perfect if we, as sinners, couldn't talk to God and Jesus. You can prove it to yourself by doing it, but you have to be really honest! God knows a fake every time! I knew then and still know now, that all my sins are forgiven. I live in great Joy every day celebrating my life and following Jesus by obeying God's Words!

God has been my
Provider, Comforter, Healer, and more
- again and again!

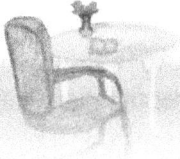

Fortune

There was a time in my life when I was homeless and jobless. I'm not going to tell the stories, at this point, of how I got there because the main thing I want everyone to know is how God got me out! I know without a doubt that God knows and is interested in and wants to be involved in every part of our lives. The qualities He has as a loving Father are shown in how He intervenes in every part of our lives.

I was living in an old farmhouse in Franklin County, VA, on twenty acres of land near Smith Mountain Lake. The house had been partially converted from a log cabin. The three rooms and back porch downstairs had walls and ceiling covered with narrow tongue and groove boards. The original curved stairway to what used to be the loft had been closed off with a door at the bottom, but it was open at the top where the floor began. The tin roof didn't completely protect the logs of the loft walls and when it snowed, the snow blew between the logs into the rooms—not a lot, but some. The outside of the farmhouse was covered with white clapboard. There was a rough, slanted porch on the front of the house and a screened porch on the back.

There was no running water on the property and no spring—only a trickle of a creek that was difficult to get even half of a bucket of water from. Of course, with no water, there was only a johnny house, but it did have electricity for light and to run an electric heater in winter. The johnny house was almost eighty feet from the farmhouse.

The farm was owned by an elderly woman friend I had known for some time. She lived in Roanoke City by herself. Her husband had been dead for a long time and her one son, who was living in Salem, VA, drove a truck so he was gone a lot. It was a twenty-five minute drive from the farmhouse to her house in the city, but I visited her often and made sure she had food to eat. I took her shopping and to doctor appointments and for walks and rides or wherever she wanted to go. She had a sister in the

1

neighborhood close enough for them to walk to see each other (until her sister died). She also had a nephew nearby, but he was too busy with his own family to do much. Other family members kept in touch regularly and two grandchildren who lived in other places occasionally visited. The entire family (several sisters, nieces, and nephews) would keep in touch.

She let me live in the farmhouse for free because I helped look after her. The house was heated with a cold morning oil stove in the middle of the living room. There was a modern electric range to cook on, as well as a small wood or coal stove for cooking, and two old refrigerators. The house was furnished with antique furniture and even an old pump organ. I had to go to the local laundromat on the way out of the area to wash towels and bed clothes, but I caught rainwater to bathe and wash small pieces of clothing by hand. Nearby churches let me fill up old milk jugs with drinking water and water for cooking. Some very nice people gave me an air conditioner because it was so hot in the summer. I was very content to be there. I spent a lot of my time crocheting baby blankets for my growing family and painting with watercolors, mowing the yard in summer, and reading and writing in winter. It was a good life, but money was in short supply.

My income was very little, but I had enough (after my tithe) for food and gas and necessities. God has always been faithful to supply my needs, but I knew I needed a job doing something when the land was passed down to other family members. When I asked God for direction, He clearly spoke to my heart to go to the L.O.A. (League of Older Americans). They suggested I go to the Virginia Employment Commission (V.E.C.) and check into help for older people going back to work. The V.E.C. connected me with Jane Fortune. She was in charge of the Title V Program, which specifically works with older people, to retrain and find jobs. After a few months of computer classes and reviewing work habits and procedures, we were employed in temporary, part-time work at minimum wage. Our instructions were to send out resumés to places of employment which interested us.

Mrs. Fortune placed me in the position of Receptionist at the Southwest Virginia U.S. Attorney's office in downtown Roanoke. I had worked a long time as receptionist in other places, so it wasn't new work for me, but all the people, names, positions, and procedures were very new, so it took a while for me to catch on and feel comfortable after so many years of not working. It was very interesting to meet all the people in the ATF, DEA, and Secret Service, plus all the Assistant U.S. Attorneys, and all the secretaries and other office personnel it took to do all the details of each organization at that office. I had to learn a lot of names and faces and a little about what they did to be able to transfer phone calls and to know when to push the "open door" button when the buzzer rang for entry. Of course, the building was also guarded by a paid security group whom I had to recognize. Then there were the mail carriers and other special deliveries and sometimes visitors from the federal courthouses and other U.S. Attorneys' offices, other attorneys, aides, temporary workers, and private citizens with or without appointments.

It was a temporary job and Mrs. Fortune continually reminded me that I had to be sending out resumés for regular employment. She said she knew I loved working there, and a lot of the employees liked having me there, but she had to go by the rules of the Title V Program. After several years of not finding a permanent job, I got a phone call from an old friend who was a counselor for a Christian counseling agency. We had kept in touch through the years, and she knew I was looking for permanent work. When there was an opening in their office for a part-time evening Intake Assistant, she called and said I should apply. The pay was still minimum wage, and it was evening work, but I really liked the people, the Christian atmosphere, and the simplicity of the work. I applied and got the job and worked until I retired at age seventy-three!

After I was employed at the Christian counseling agency for about two years, Jane Fortune, who had been the L.O.A. Title V Supervisor, came to work as a Counselor. To me, it was confirmation from God that I was employed where He wanted me to be. I wasn't making a "fortune," but I was where God placed me, within a Christian atmosphere and where I could freely witness my faith in God.

Thank You, Jesus!

Paradise

The job Jane Fortune found for me at the U.S. Attorney's office in Roanoke, VA, was a wonderful answer to my prayer to God for help with my finances, even though it was only a "temporary" part-time job to retrain me. Driving the long distance between the office and the farmhouse was taking a lot of time, plus wear on my already aging car. My elderly friend had been letting me live at the farmhouse in exchange for caring for her. My prayer to God this time was to help me find a place to live closer to work.

One day a "For Sale" sign appeared at a gravel driveway up a little hill surrounded by trees and bushes. I couldn't see the house, but it didn't matter because I knew I couldn't buy a house. My job wasn't permanent, and my income wasn't enough. The only good things about my situation were: I didn't owe anyone any money, I had excellent credit, and I had managed to save $500! I don't even remember how I had managed to do that! I argued with God when I kept feeling the urge to drive up that little hill . . . just to see what was there. I said:

> *"Father God, You know I can't buy a house! I don't even have a permanent job and I'm only working 20 hours a week at minimum wage! I can't buy a house!"*

But one day, my car seemed to decide, itself, to go up that hill! I was so surprised and excited over what I saw! a small, redwood cabin with a tin roof (which I love), and a covered front porch (to hang up a big porch swing), and the sun shining on a deck in the back! It was surrounded by huge trees that blocked out any view of the neighbors. The back yard slanted downhill on the north side, and then dropped almost straight down to a tiny creek between the property and a beautiful three-story house with a paved driveway

5

behind me. A large cow pasture was to the west, the main road to the next county was on the south, and a tiny house hidden by trees was to the east. I couldn't believe this hidden treasure was only two and a half miles from the U.S. Attorney's office!

I could tell no one lived there, so I got out of my car and went up on the front porch to peek in the window. Hardwood floors! I love hardwood floors! As I looked around through the window, I could see a wood stove, and I got so excited I said, "Yes, this is where I want to live!" Imagine! A cabin in the woods, next to a farm, only two and a half miles from work, with a tin roof, a deck, a covered front porch with hooks for a porch swing, and a wood stove. A real cabin with running water and an indoor bathroom! It was perfect . . . but I had no idea how I could possibly buy a house. Only God could work out that miracle.

I wrote down the realtor's name, Paradis. I called her, and we met soon after. I told her I had worked as a receptionist for over twenty years, had good credit, no debts, and was employed at the U.S. Attorney's office part-time, temporary. I had $500 saved, and my son and his wife gave me $5000 to help. Somehow, she got me the loan! I had talked to God and told Him if I was supposed to buy it, He would help the loan go through. It did! *Thank you, Jesus!*

So many people gave me furniture and appliances and helped me move in. My children were skeptical of the purchase, but I knew in my heart it was right for me. I think they thought being sixty-three was too old to buy a house, but I have been here twenty plus years now, and at eighty-four I am healthier than I was twenty years ago! (That's another story!) My house payment may be one of the lowest in the U.S.A.!

Beginning in 1999 when I moved into my "paradise," I have been living in Glorious Victory! Because of the miracles of Fortune and Paradise, no one can refute the truth of the fact that I am completely forgiven! I feel so blessed and so loved by God! He went to special extremes to make sure I knew I was forgiven. He has given me a whole new life since I moved into His house, joined the church, and went to work at the Christian counseling agency (from which I retired in 2008).

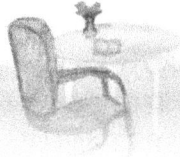

The Gift Card

I had met a young couple at the church I was attending who had just had their first baby, a boy, and were now ministering at their first church in the country about thirty miles from Roanoke in Eagle Rock. I was their friend, a mentor, and excited over their new baby and their first opportunity to pastor a church. I decided to make the trip to hear him preach one Sunday. I hadn't been in my new little cabin very long and hadn't really settled down in a church in my new neighborhood.

It was a very bright, sunny day and a beautiful drive through the countryside as I drove home after the service. There was practically no traffic on the road, the area was fairly flat, and the sky seemed huge, with no tall city buildings to block the view. All of a sudden, the inside of my car got even brighter! Then the area right around the front of my car also got very bright! I can't remember if I stopped or not, but I knew it was the Presence of God, even though I had never experienced anything like that before! I didn't hear an audible voice, but God spoke directly into my heart. He said:

"Shirley, this is a 'Gift Card' to you."

I didn't know what to think, and I didn't want to appear stupid, but I had to be honest. I knew it had to be God, so I said, "I don't know what You mean." God answered:

*I gave you a **job***
*Through a woman named **FORTUNE***
*And a **house***
*Through a woman named **PARADIS***

Job = Fortune
& Home = Paradise

"You can go around all the world and you will not find another person this has happened to."

7

God explained to me that the "Gift Card" was for me to share Fortune and Paradise as proof that all my sins were paid in full by Jesus!

I was shocked! I still did not understand the phrase "This is a Gift Card to you," but I was so astounded I didn't even remember the drive home! I've told this story many times and am still amazed that God, Himself, has taken such a personal interest in my life and that now I have proof He hears and answers my prayers and is involved in every area of my life! It is comforting to know He cares about everything I do and is meeting my every need. He is really treating me like He IS My Father, and I am His Little Child!

Later, when I was telling this story to my head deacon at our church, he explained to me that you "Redeem" a "Gift Card" by using it.

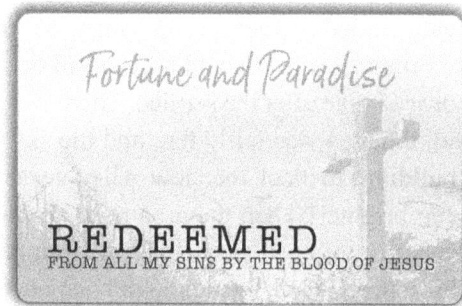

I feel such joy in my heart because every time I tell this story I am telling of my Redemption from sin—that Jesus has paid for all my sins, and I am Redeemed! It is also an evangelism tool to let others know they can be Redeemed by Jesus' blood!

"I know where you live and everything you do."
—II KINGS 19:27 NET

Thank You, Jesus!
Praise Your Name!

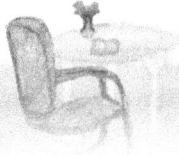

Baptism of The Holy Spirit

This is a simple story just to tell how God, Himself, has been so involved in my life. The amazing thing about this story is that God cares about each person so much that He guides us through every day if we listen to His soft voice speaking to our hearts. I'm not trying to become rich and famous. I just want to tell my stories so other people can know God like I know Him. This isn't going to be a chronological record of my life, but a record of how God intervened in my life in times of need.

In 1971, the night before I was scheduled to have a hysterectomy, I was reading a book by David Wilkerson called *The Cross and The Switchblade*. In all my years of being raised in a Southern Baptist Church—in a Christian family whose history/genealogy included the strict German Baptist or Brethren (sometimes called Dunkard) teaching—I never learned anything about being "baptized in The Holy Spirit". I was absolutely enthralled by the complete change made in the lives of the people who had experienced this in the book. I read in my Bible where Jesus said He would baptize with The Holy Spirit, but I didn't know what that meant. I remember one time as a young teen, I asked about the Trinity and who the Holy Spirit was, but the teacher said she could not explain it.

I was thirty-five years old when I got on my knees at the window on the 8th floor of Roanoke Memorial Hospital and had the most real conversation with God I had ever had. I told Him I realized I could die during surgery because my body was so sensitive to any amount of medication. (One time after surgery, the nurses had a difficult time waking me from anesthesia and I almost left this life.) So, I was concerned that I really might not wake up this time.

I told God I wasn't sure I would come to heaven, that I had sinned and hurt people and couldn't go back and undo all the wrong things

I had done. I did believe that God, through His Holy Spirit, could go to each person and heal any hurt that I had caused, so I asked Him to please do that. I also asked Him to baptize me in His Holy Spirit, even though I wasn't sure what that meant or what would happen in my life.

I remember feeling euphoric when I finished praying! I got up and went to bed without any fear. I came through the surgery fine. I knew that, not only was I now physically healthier, but clearly something different was happening in my heart and mind. I realized that the Lord had, indeed, baptized me with His Holy Spirit, because the first thing I wanted to do was to go to a Christian bookstore and buy a new Bible!

" 'Heaven and earth will pass away,
but my words will never pass away.' "
—MATTHEW 24:35 NET

Newspapers

Are the kids and I supposed to deliver newspapers?
The Miracle of God's answer to my prayer.

I 'm not going to try, at this time, to explain the difficulties of my first marriage. Like everybody's life, it was complicated. I remember the day vividly. I was sitting in the red, upholstered, plush rocking chair and my children's father was standing at the open closet door in our bedroom. Our son was half-sitting/half-standing leaning against me. We watched as he grabbed clothes off the hangers and stuffed everything into a suitcase. The only words I remember him saying were: "I don't want to live in a house with a bunch of Christians!" So many times, since that day, I have wondered if our son thought his Daddy was leaving because he had just been baptized a week before. I'm not going into the details of all the financial trouble that followed. I'm just going to say it was difficult, but I learned to trust God and He sent Christian people to help.

Although I never received any money from my ex-husband, he gave me our home plus two rental properties. I was determined that I would not have him arrested for not paying child support because I didn't want my children thinking it was my fault if he was in jail for non-support. I felt like they had enough to deal with. The one good thing to come out of this situation was we learned how to pray to God and depend on His help for every need. When I finally realized that their father wasn't going to pay his child support, my prayer life really came alive for the first time in my life. Necessity *is* the Best Teacher!

I talked to myself and to God about what to do about more money. I was employed full-time as a Dental Assistant. My employer was a strong Christian and helped me grow spiritually by introducing me to the Catholic Charismatic Movement (late 60's/early 70's). He invited me to go with his family to prayer meetings and I grew closer and closer to the Lord than I had ever been before. I learned how to really get in touch with God. I also received the gift of tongues, which I had never heard of in the Southern Baptist Church I was raised in. I learned about being "born again" (John 3:3 NKJV), being "baptized in Holy Spirit" (Acts 11:16 NKJV), and that miracles do still happen to people who believe! It was an exciting, even though difficult, time and my faith grew by leaps and bounds!

One morning after the children had left for school and as I was preparing to go out the door to work, I had another prayer with God. This time it was about money. I had spent part of the night thinking about a second job either before or after my dental assistant job. I thought maybe I could be a waitress at an early morning breakfast restaurant or even after work. I decided against working after the kids got out of school because I wouldn't be with them for the evening meal and after-school activities. Both girls were in the band and my son had sports practice and events. That only left early mornings for a job.

Then I remembered that I had helped my brother deliver papers a few times when we were about twelve and fourteen years old. I thought it would be a good thing for the children to take turns every third morning so they could all feel like they were helping. Plus, it would be good training in working any job and everyone would feel like they were contributing. I decided to petition God specifically about a paper route. I told Him I didn't have a husband to help me make decisions, and He would have to "be my husband" and tell me "yes" or "no" about delivering newspapers before work and school.

I had heard several preachers say not to pick up the Bible and just open it for an answer, but I was desperate for help from God and told Him I really needed an answer about what to do. My Bible I had at that time was the one I had bought after my prayer to receive the baptism of The Holy Spirit before my surgery. It was The New English Bible (and not what I would now call one of the best translations), but it was all I had. I held it up and said, "Okay, Father God, I'm going to trust You to tell me what to do," and I opened it up. It opened to the book of Esther. I thought, *"Oh! No! Nobody reads Esther!"* (Those were my exact words!—because *I* had never read Esther!) The heading at the top of page 556 was:

"Haman's downfall and Mordecai's triumph."
"That night sleep eluded the King, so he ordered the chronicle of daily events to be brought. . ."
—ESTHER 6:1 NEB

I could hardly believe my eyes! It sounded like a modern-day newspaper to me! I had heard of newspapers being called "The Chronicle," and "Daily Events" would be like our daily newspapers today where we read of what is taking place around the world. I was so excited that God actually spoke to me by answering my prayer! And I'm still excited after all these years!

I called the paper delivery office to set up a meeting, and within a few days we were on our way with a new family project. It took great discipline, patience, and attention to details to deliver 200 papers. Not only did we have to make sure to get to the correct address, but each customer also had a requested delivery spot. Then there was the financial part: who owed how much and when to collect, depending on the customer's schedule.

My three children learned early how to work and do the job right while keeping the customers happy. My son has worked since he was 11 years old. He took over the entire paper route, including the collecting, when he was thirteen years old. He rode a bicycle and strengthened his leg muscles enough to be on the track team in high school. When he wanted to go somewhere, he rode his bike or just ran. He's still running at fifty-nine.

When God gave us the paper route, He didn't just provide a way for us to have food and gas money, but He used that experience to teach my children how to be responsible workers: honest, dependable, hardworking, and disciplined in every way. All three worked their way through college, without financial help from their parents. My oldest daughter graduated *magna cum laude* with a major and a minor; my second daughter graduated with a master's; and my son graduated with a double major.

When I told God He was going to have to "be my husband" to help me make decisions about the finances, I didn't even think about Him also being a "Father" to my three children, but that is exactly what happened! They learned to pray and ask Him for help and guidance, also. I'm still amazed at how God pays attention to the smallest details of our lives!

HE IS ALIVE!!!

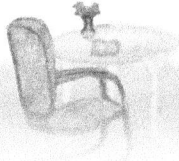

Life or Death
Stage 4 Breast Cancer—Hospice to Healed

On February 16 (my son's birthday), 2009, I was sitting in the breast cancer surgeon's office, and the surgeon told me I had stage four inflammatory breast cancer. He explained that it was difficult to heal, I was dying, and I would not be around for my son's next birthday. (I already suspected I had breast cancer. Actually, when I was eighteen, my left breast began to drain a little, and a specialist told me not to nurse my babies. So, the cancer probably began early in my life.) He further told me I needed surgery, chemotherapy, and radiation—but even at that, he couldn't promise success, because at that time they didn't have a very successful protocol for that type of breast cancer. I told him I couldn't decide right then if I was even going to have treatment. I explained that I was a Christian and needed to go home and talk to my Heavenly Father and see what He wanted me to do. I tell people about my prayer which was:

> *"Father God, this is Your child, Shirley. You heard the cancer surgeon tell me I have stage 4 breast cancer and that I will die without their treatment plan. Father, I am already seventy-three years old, and have my three children and 10 grandchildren. I have traveled all through Europe, gone on two mission trips to India, have seen the U.S. from northern Maine to Florida and the eastern states to the Mississippi, and have done a lot of wonderful things—so I am ready to come home to Heaven to see You if it is my time. I know Jesus paid for my sins when He died on the cross, so I know Heaven's door is open for me. But! If You still have something else You want me to do, You will have to heal me, Yourself, because I am not going to have surgery or chemo or radiation."*

It takes a great deal of faith and intervention from the hand of God to do what I decided to do. I was ready to die—meaning:

I knew my heart was cleansed of all sin by the blood of Jesus Christ when He died on the cross. I knew my Father God loved me and has forgiven me of all my sin—past, present, and future—and I had already received eternal life when I was a child of eight.

I was filled with His Holy Spirit when I was thirty-five (even though I turned away from Him for three and a half years during my mid-life crisis). I could never lose my salvation.

God forgives all sin if you ask!

When I called the surgeon and told him I was not going to take any treatment, he said, "Well, you are dying, so you need to go to your family doctor so they can set you up with Hospice." I made an appointment with my family doctor. As she was reading the information on the computer, without looking at me even once, she said: "With the type of cancer you have, you have less than six months to live. We need to set you up with Hospice. So, which Hospice would you like?" I said, "Gentle Shepherd" (because one of my daughters worked with that agency).

My oldest daughter decided we needed one last "bonding" time, so she arranged for the two of us to go to the beach for a weekend. It truly was a great trip! When I got back, I continued to get all of my affairs in order.

Gentle Shepherd began visiting me immediately. They were wonderful people, and it was a comforting thing to have Christian medical people coming to my home three–four times a week. However, Father God had a different plan. Instead of getting weaker and sicker, He healed me! I just watched the cancer go away until there were no lumps, no swelling, and no inflammation—and I felt well! Amazing! Two or three months later, I had to call Hospice and tell them to stop coming. I didn't need them anymore. They had done a fantastic job, But:

God healed me!
My cancer was gone!
and I felt GREAT!

That was over ten years ago. HALLELUJAH! I haven't been to any doctor in ten years and take no medications for anything—and I am eighty-four. I eat a healthy diet, get lots of exercise, have a peaceful attitude about life and death, and am excited every day because He does have something else for me to do—several somethings. Instead of dying, The Lord Jesus has given me:

1) World Prayer Ministry
2) Mission Field on Mill Mountain
3) Ask Ministry at my church (counseling and praying for people)
4) 2020 Vision (from Acts 20:20—more later!)

I am amazed at my life and what God has done and I want to share my joy with everyone!

And . . . knowing you are about to die *is* a life-changing experience—even if you are already sure you are going to Heaven! Of course, planning your own funeral and deciding how to leave an inheritance is part of the process; but, how to spend my last days was more important. Time becomes very precious. It is too bad we don't realize early in life that time is always very valuable. How we spend every moment has a great effect on, not just our own future, but the lives of every person we interact with. *What we think guides what we do!*

It's our thinking that keeps us united with God; and it's our thinking that affects every relationship, regardless of the length of time spent in that relationship. Even a short-term encounter—just a person passing through our lives as we go about doing our daily activities—could be a divine appointment to see Jesus or be that very person that someone else needs at that exact moment. Admitting our sinfulness and our need for a Savior—Jesus—is absolutely necessary as we live our days! We do need to get our affairs in order. We do need to settle our funeral arrangements to relieve a difficult burden of our loved ones. And, we certainly *do* need to settle our "Going Home" with Father God. If you don't know Father God—personally—take a few minutes to talk with Him now.

Note: I believed I should verify my healing with the cancer surgeon, so I did go back to see him one year after my healing. He verified that the cancer was gone. He checked me out and said, "You're right! It's gone!" My medical record is in 4 medical offices, including Gentle Shepherd Hospice.

Mill Mountain Star
Missionary at 80!

The story of how I became a World Missionary on top of Mill Mountain at the Star Overlook is amazing! I am one of the granddaughters of Lula Kinsey, who is a sister of Roy C. Kinsey, Sr., who owned the sign company that designed the "World's Largest Man-made Star"—as the sign on Mill Mountain says: www.visitroanokeva.com/things-to-do/attractions/roanoke-star.

I remember when they turned the Star on for the first time in 1949. Daddy was so excited for Uncle Roy and his three boys (Daddy's cousins): Roy Jr., Warren, and Bobby designing the Star and building all the neon tubing for it, that the night they flipped the electric switch to turn on the lights in the Star, he got us (the three oldest children) and a flashlight and said: "We're going to climb up Green Ridge to see the Star turn on for the first time!" So, we were there when the lights in the Star were turned on for the first time on November 23, 1949. It was a great surprise for us!

Of course, living in Roanoke County most of my life, the Star has been a special place to visit for a panoramic view of Roanoke and the mountains that surround it. It also acts as a guide and landmark to most people who live here. The thing that stands out most in my mind is that when we were returning from a trip somewhere, we knew we were home when we saw the Star.

I have gone to the Star off and on through the years. One day I decided to drive up Mill Mountain to see the Star, again; it had been a long time since I had been there. I was walking the paved pathway from the top of the Mountain to the Discovery Center and zoo area, when I came across three people: a middle-aged man, his wife, and a second woman who I think was not a daughter, but a friend. I spoke and we began to chat a little bit. The younger woman suddenly burst

19

into tears—sobbing with every breath! The man stepped away, and I put my arms around the one crying and asked, "May I pray with you?" She and the other woman both said, "Yes!" So I prayed to the Lord for His hand to be on their lives and to bring healing and peace. That was the beginning of my "Mission on the Mountain".

God spoke to my heart and said:

"This is your Mission Field
and I am going to send the people to you!"

I really didn't understand exactly what that meant, but I started going more often (that was in the latter part of 2015). I tell them my Kinsey cousins built the Star when I was a child. Then I tell them how God healed me of stage four inflammatory breast cancer. I had refused treatment and prepared to die. But God miraculously healed me! I come now almost every day, unless the weather is too frigid or rainy. I pray as to what time to come, stay as long as the Holy Spirit says, and talk to whomever He has here for me to talk to. I pray every time, all the way up the Mountain, that Jesus Himself would use me (my body, my voice, and my love for people that He put in me) just to tell my story to those who will listen. Since I am obviously an older woman and non-threatening looking, most people are open to listening.

In 1989, my second daughter gave me a book called *Operation World* by Jason Mandryk and Patrick Johnstone. (She had been teaching her children from the child's version.) Her gift was perfect! I have wanted to be a missionary since I was a teenager but didn't know how to become one. I married at eighteen, lived in France two years and enjoyed visiting other countries. We made trips all over France wherever we could find old castles that were open to public visits. We also went to Belgium, Luxembourg, Liechtenstein, The Netherlands and across the English Channel on a ferry boat to visit London, Stratford-upon-Avon, Cambridge, Nottingham and then over the Pyrenees Mountains, through Andorra into Barcelona, Spain. These visits whet my appetite to see the world; but since I never had the opportunity to do much traveling (other than my two mission trips to India) after my time in France, the *Operation World* book opened the whole world up to me in a very different way.

Operation World is a prayer guide manual that lists one country or area per day in alphabetical order. It gives a small outline map of the area's geographical location and important statistics such as: people groups, languages, religion, and politics. Most importantly, it gives a list of the most urgent prayer concerns for that particular area. So, in 1989 I began using this wonderful book to pray for the world, one country at a time. I followed the guidelines for days of prayer and specific information concerning what to pray about. If I came to a country that appeared to have little or no Christian witness, I would tell the Lord: "Oh, God, I wish I could go there and learn that language and tell those people about Your Son, Jesus, who died on that cross to pay for their sins."

Five *Operation World* books and thirty years later, I am still praying for the world! I have developed a little bit of knowledge that helps me understand the news reports I hear. I also developed a great love for all people and a desire that they know Jesus Christ as their Savior. God heard my prayers and knew the longing of my heart to be a missionary to go everywhere! Of course, I'm much older now, and lack of funds keeps me at home—that is, until God said:

*"Mill Mountain is going to be YOUR Mission Field
and I am going to send the people to you!"*

As a child growing up, I was so shy and quiet and fairly uncomfortable around strangers because I didn't really know how to talk to people for a long time. Eventually, after years in church I was able to take part in discussions; in my Dental Assistant career I was compelled to be friendly to strangers; and secretarial jobs where I was a receptionist I had to talk to people I didn't know. Finally, I feel free within myself to talk to whomever God directs me to.

On the Mountain, I began to just greet people with questions about whether they live in Roanoke, or where they are from, and if this is their first visit to the Star. I quickly discovered that not only are many of the visitors from all across the United States, but they are from all over the world! I began writing down the countries of foreign visitors and have been astounded by the fact that people come to Roanoke, Virginia, just to visit the "World's Largest Man-Made Star" from everywhere.

My oldest daughter gave me a copy of Jason Mandryk's book *Pray for the World* the Christmas of 2017. It is an abridged version of *Operation World, 7th edition*, so it is much easier for me to carry and has been so helpful as I meet people and can make a quick search about their country. In the twenty-seven months (and counting!) that I have been, almost daily, going to the Star, I have witnessed to people from one hundred and nineteen countries! (*Operation World* lists two hundred and twenty-eight countries, mega-cities, and islands in the world.) God has transformed this shy farm girl, without a college degree, and without enough money to pay for a cab to the airport (much less buy a ticket to fly anywhere) into a World Missionary because I have proven to our Heavenly Father that I really care about the "lost" of this world through my thirty plus years of prayer.

I'm a World Missionary six miles from home!

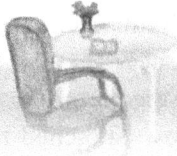

Back Story
My Kinsey Cousins

A little back story on Daddy's side of the family. The Kinseys were the creators of the Mill Mountain Star. My Daddy's mother, Grandma (Lula), was a Kinsey before she married Papa (John Jackson Morgan). Papa was from North Carolina (that's all I remember anyone in my family telling me specifically about him). He was injured in a war, but I don't recall hearing which war or what area of service he was in or what his injury was or what kind of work he did. My Daddy was so sick for so long, I never thought to ask him. The Kinsey family is from the Burnt Chimney area of Franklin County. (One time I was able to find an old graveyard with some of my paternal grandmother's family on the farm of a nice couple, who gave their approval for my access to the grave site.) Of Uncle Roy and Aunt Macye's three boys, I remember the youngest boy, Bobby, the best. I really liked Aunt Macye. She had snow-white hair all fluffy around her face, and always had a small ribbon in her hair, but her most outstanding quality was her laughter! She seemed to laugh all the time and I liked her so much I decided I wanted to be like her when I grew up—a ribbon in my hair and always laughing, instead of being grumpy like a lot of other older people I had met.

Uncle Roy, as we kids all called Roy Kinsey, Sr., was very outstanding, himself. To us kids he was like a cowboy hero from the movies! He was tall and big with a boisterous voice, and completely took over every "scene" he was in! He wore cowboy boots and a white Stetson hat and drove a new, white Cadillac. He could have walked right off a Gene Autry movie set as far as I was concerned! I was just a little kid, but my memory is sharp about him. My Daddy must have really admired him because every time Uncle Roy did anything new on his huge farm, Daddy put us four kids and Mama in the car and took us up to see—even if it was just a new calf that had been born! I still have the picture in my mind of the first time I saw Uncle Roy's milk cows attached to electric milkers. I also have a clear memory of looking at the machines that separated the cream from the milk. When pasteurization became mandatory for people who sold milk, off we went to Uncle Roy's farm. Everything Uncle Roy did was a big deal to my Daddy, which helped me see his own dreams for the future of his little farm. I'm sure he dreamed of doing the same things Uncle Roy did, but his health interrupted all his dreams of a big farming operation. I'm sure he questioned God about why he got so sick so young and why his eyesight failed in his 40's! I wonder, myself, but I also remember what he did accomplish. He was a good Christian, faithful in church and modeled that to his children. His silly jokes, fun trips, and enjoyment of western movies, and all the time he spent babysitting my children and forming a strong bond with them is his legacy.

Uncle Roy's farm was right next to Roanoke City, near what is now Roanoke-Blacksburg Regional Airport. Roanoke City built a highway that may have even taken part of the farm. Eventually, the old homeplace became the site of Countryside Golf Course (it closed in 2010). You can't tell there was ever a large dairy cow and horse farm with huge barns, tenant houses, and peacocks strutting around in the yard. There were even Palomino horses he had brought in from Texas! I was just a small child when the peacocks were there, but the memory of those huge, beautiful birds is still in my mind! I know my own Daddy wanted to be like his Uncle Roy, but life got difficult while he was still fairly young. Even though he worked and worked his own small piece of land, he still had his dream for all the open land around our farm that Grandma and Papa owned. Daddy spent a lot of time drawing plans for his and Mama's dream retirement home on a little knoll. He built several barns and sheds for our pigs and chickens, and a playhouse for us kids! He was always so patient with me and my million questions, even though I was right under his feet in everything he did. One of the things he taught me was how to care for the rabbits. He stressed fresh water every day, and in summer to be sure to pick fresh green leaves from the yard (a special kind), and to not put my hand in the nest when Mama Rabbit was in it. When he put two big rabbits in one pen, I asked him why he did that. I was so very innocent for a long time that I still didn't understand why—even when some baby rabbits appeared one day. I was also the child who was given the job of slopping the hogs (carrying the leftover food to the hog pen) because I wasn't afraid of the dark. Amazing!

I got to talk a lot to God when I was outside.

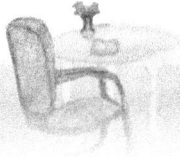

Mountaintop Art

After I had been witnessing for several months on Mill Mountain, I was going through my artwork at home. In the 90s and early 2000s I finally had time to do some serious painting. I never had art lessons, sold a painting, or had an art show. I told myself I wasn't good enough, so I just packed them away in a big plastic tub in my art room. One day I got them out and was looking at them. They looked better than I had remembered. God had told me to put Bible verses on my paintings and call them my *Memorial Paintings*. So, desiring to always be obedient, I prayed over each one to choose a verse that complemented the painting. As I looked at them, I thought: "What am I going to do with all these paintings?" Then I told myself to just put them away because all my kids, grandkids, and great-grandkids would divide them up. I put them back in the plastic tub, put the lid on, and walked out of my hobby room into the living room, and God plainly spoke to my heart:

> *"Shirley, take your art to the print shop and make copies and take them to Mill Mountain and give them away!"*

I thought: "My Goodness! What a good idea!" So, I did what God said to do. I still didn't realize the full intent of what God was doing until one day on the Mountain when I was telling my stories to a woman who had picked out a painting. I rolled it loosely with a rubber band and handed it to her quickly because she was in a hurry to get to the airport. After she left, I had a sudden insight into what was happening. I gave a painting with a Bible verse on it to a woman who was on her way to catch a plane to fly back to her home in Russia! I thought, "Oh, my goodness! My painting, with God's Words, is on its way to Russia! Father God, You are making me a World Missionary! I'm still in awe of what God is doing in my life!"

On another day, I was talking with five people from Ethiopia: three women and two men, who were here in the U.S. on vacation. The youngest woman said: "I'm fifty years old," and then pointing, she said: "That's my mother. She is seventy years old," and pointing to the third woman she said: "That's my grandmother. She is ninety years old!" I told her about my paintings, and she was very excited to see them. I led them all to my car and laid my portfolio on the trunk, and the mother and daughter began looking through the paintings. Everyone was talking at once and I was trying to keep up with the conversations, as they each looked at all of my paintings. I wasn't paying any attention to the men who were also involved in looking at my paintings. When they all got to the end, they closed the portfolio and began to walk away. I was stunned! I said, "Don't you want any paintings?" "They are free!" The younger woman said, "Oh, my husband photographed all your paintings!" I knew they had been talking to each other in their language; but, of course, I had no idea what they were saying. I got really excited then! When I called my oldest daughter and told her my story, she exclaimed, "Mama! They are going to take your paintings and sell them in Ethiopia and make a million dollars!" I said, "Good! I hope they make two or three million dollars! My paintings with God's Words are going all over Ethiopia!" I told my pastor on Sunday what had happened, I said, "Ethiopia may have a revival before we have one in the U.S.!" (I hope so!) My mission is to get God's Word around the world!

I don't remember which countries or how many of my paintings have gone where. I'm not trying to keep track. I'm just blessed beyond measure that God has allowed me to be part of His work around the world. I just feel wonderfully Blessed! God knew when He created me that I was going to be an artist. (I inherited the Kinsey art gene.) He deliberately had me born as a cousin, into the Star family (the Kinseys), and old enough to remember when it was turned on the first time. God also gave me a heart that cared for other people from the time I was a child. I've never been a racist; God gave me His love for all people. He had me born into a Christian family, whose ancient history included the Dunkards, which is a strict religious sect that dunked people sitting in a chair to baptize them. My immediate family was and still is Southern Baptist, and I am so grateful for my father's determination and dependability when it came to worship—twice on Sunday and Wednesday night prayer meeting. Being raised in the country, on a small farm in Roanoke County, with a modest income, was the best thing that could have happened to me. It kept me innocent of the wickedness of the fast-paced city life and gave me a great love for the God who created all the things of nature that I grew to love, plus I experienced the peace and quiet that is a large part of my attachment to God's world. I realized soon after God said that Mill Mountain was going to be my "Mission Field," that Caleb, who was with Moses from the beginning of *The Exodus* from Egypt, asked God *"give him this mountain,"* when he was eighty-five and *"he destroyed the giants there."* I pray I am also destroying the "giants" of sin in the lives of people I pray for!

> (Caleb) *" 'And now, behold, the Lord has kept me alive, as He said, these forty-five years, ever since the Lord spoke this word to Moses while Israel wandered in the wilderness; and now, here I am this day, eighty-five years old. As yet I am as strong this day as on the day that Moses sent me; just as my strength was then, so now is my strength for war, both for going out and for coming in. Now therefore, give me this mountain of which the Lord spoke in that day; for you heard in that day how the Anakim were there, and that the cities were great and fortified. It may be that the Lord will be with me, and I shall be able to drive them out as the Lord said.' "*
> —JOSHUA 14:10–12 NKJV

WHAT A BLESSING!

2020 VISION
NO FEAR

I remember clearly when the Boston Bombing occurred that I just stood shocked, dumbfounded, angry and afraid in the middle of my living room, and said out loud to God:

"Father God! What are we supposed to do in America? We keep having shootings and bombings! Everyone is going to be afraid to go to sporting events, movie theaters, music events, dining, amusement parks, or any community events! Americans are going to be afraid to gather in crowds anywhere! What can I do, Lord?"

I had no idea when I asked Him that question that He was going to answer me so quickly! But He immediately spoke right to my heart. God said:

"Every Christian is responsible to know if their neighbors have heard the Gospel of Jesus Christ."

(I had heard someone say that the perpetrators of one terrorist attack actually lived, either in their apartment building or next door, and how shocked they were to learn there were terrorists living so close by.)

Then God directed me to a story in the Bible about King Hezekiah:

"And Hezekiah sent to all Israel and Judah, and also wrote letters to Ephraim and Manasseh, that they should come to the house of the Lord at Jerusalem, to keep the Passover to the Lord God of Israel."
—II CHRONICLES 30:1 NKJV

God said to send information out all over the U.S.A., calling people to Bible study. He directed me to an organization called Every Home for Christ, that I had heard about for years. They had just published a 52-week study book called *Be Fruitful and Multiply*. This study is now *The Discovery Method* and can be found at *https://everyhome. org/get-involved/discovery-method/*. They allow anyone to download information from their website to teach home Bible studies. God's idea is to have a Bible study in every neighborhood in America to be sure our neighbors know Jesus Christ.

After much prayer and direction from the Lord, I went to a Christian printing company and the owner/printer designed a brochure for the *2020 Vision* project: AR_2T or *America's Response 2 Terrorism*. God guided me to choose *one* city from each state (except Hawaii) each month, and four churches in each city, and mail the AR_2T brochure, plus a *2020 Vision* flyer for year 2020, using *Acts 20:20* where Paul wrote that he

> ". . . *taught you publicly and from house to house,*"
> —ACTS 20:20 NKJV

The Lord made it clear to me He wanted Bible studies in every neighborhood across the U.S.A. He said:

> "*You have seven years, from 2013–2019,*
> *to mail out this information for a Revival in 2020.*"

It is 2018 as I am writing this. I am in year #6 and 2019 will be year #7. I have mailed thousands of the AR_2T brochures and *2020 Vision* flyers across the U.S.A. and am confidently looking for Revival beginning in 2020! *Because God said so!*

God so arranged my limited finances to be able to do this entire project: paying for the printing of brochures and flyers, buying envelopes and stamps, folding and stuffing, and using the local library computer to find church names and addresses so I could hand-address each one myself. I feel blessed beyond measure! Caleb was eighty-five when he took his mountain! I was eighty when I began witnessing on top of Mill Mountain as my Mission Field. I said, *"Lord, like Caleb, give me this mountain!"* and He did!

I have been praying and working daily for Revival in 2020 for the United States of America! I need all the prayer-helpers I can get to turn this great nation back to God! We began this country with God. Our laws and Constitution are from The Great Creator, God, and His Son, Jesus Christ. We need to acknowledge this truth again and give Him the Honor and Glory He is due!

Having had cancer and preparing to die ten years ago was a time of personal renewal, but it also brought a pressing *desire of my heart* for the world to know my story and to wake up America to the fact that none of us know when or how we will die . . . but we have less time today than we had yesterday or last year.

It is time to decide what to do with the rest of your life!

Jesus Christ, the Son of God, came to earth as a man, to die on a cross, to pay the Sin-Debt of every person who will just *ask* Him to be their Savior. It is as simple as that! He is listening and waiting on *you* because God loves *you*!

Note: I could not *possibly* have known in 2013, when God gave me these instructions, that in 2020 **everyone** in the **entire world** would be behind the doors of their own homes **during Passover just like II Chronicles 30**!

> *"And Hezekiah sent to all Israel and Judah, and also wrote letters to Ephraim and Manasseh, that they should come to the house of the Lord at Jerusalem, to keep the Passover to the Lord God of Israel."*
> — II CHRONICLES 30:1 NKJV

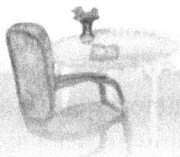

India Missions
Scripture for Life

In 1994, I went on a short-term mission trip to India. The one thing that profoundly affected me, was an encounter with a man who I believe was an angel sent by God. I was sitting in a large dining room one morning, waiting for our first group activity, when a man from across the room got up and walked right to my table. All he said was:

"There are two verses of Scripture you need to live by."

He gave the references, and quoted the Scriptures, and left (or vanished!). I have no memory of watching where he went. Those two Scriptures completely changed my life. The most important one to me was:

". . . and bringing into captivity every thought
to the obedience of Christ . . ."
—II Corinthians 10:5 KJV

I began, at that moment, learning how to do that. It has been twenty-four years now and that Scripture has taught me, daily, how to get sin out of my life. It was difficult at first, to remember to catch every ugly thought before Satan could use it to drag me into sin; but I can tell you now, after all these years, what cleansing power it has had on my life!

The second Scripture the stranger (angel) in India gave me was:

". . . know we no man after the flesh . . ."
—II Corinthians 5:16 KJV

35

For me, particularly at that time, and in that place, it was a warning against the advances of men, especially one man, with whom I began to have difficulty immediately. It took a lot of intense prayer to hear God's voice about how to react and what to say when I was sexually harassed. It wasn't an open, embarrassing, public attack, but subtle and, from people watching, but not hearing, seemingly just another private chat. However, the chat was much more personal and intimate. He didn't use specific words, but I was extremely uncomfortable because I knew the intent of them. I prayed and kept my cool and steered the conversation in another direction. I had to do that several more times before the trip home. He didn't leave me alone, even after I came back to the U.S. and went back to work. The end of that story, after some difficult encounters, was that he finally gave up and left me alone. The stranger (angel) who told me to live by II Corinthians 5:16 must have had special insight from God. That verse has helped me deal with all kinds of people on every level of interaction, because I learned how to pray, in every situation in life, and how to allow The Holy Spirit to lead me in how to deal with other people. Of course, I'm still learning on a daily basis how to use both of these important Scriptures!

Un-Christian Responses

After I returned home from India, on two separate occasions in Bible study groups when I gave my testimony about the encounter with the stranger in India, I got very shocking, un-Christian responses. I learned that not everyone is receptive to the things of God. I only shared the first Scripture about capturing the thoughts we have moment by moment, so we can get sin out of our lives. I told of the intense battle being a long hard fight against Satan, but that finally, after years of practice, I am now able to keep sinful thoughts out of my head. Of course, Satan still does the attacking, but we aren't sinning until we begin to dwell on whatever he is trying to get us to toy with in our minds. *"Capturing my thoughts"* has not only cleansed my mind from lustful thinking, but it has given me the ability to stop anger and judgment against other people. It has also opened up my thought life to almost constant prayer with God! I have to have His power to live this way, so I need to keep my conversation with Him going all the time! II Corinthians 10:5 is the path to Isaiah 26:3! It can be done!

> *"You will keep him in perfect peace, Whose mind is stayed on You, Because he trusts in You."*
> —ISAIAH 26:3 NKJV

Both times that I shared this testimony in Bible study, I was greatly assailed by some of the women who called me self-righteous! I was completely shocked by their reaction to what seemed to me to be a wonderful victory over sin. I shared my story to give hope and passion and direction to others who, I thought, wanted to get sin out of their lives, too. Instead of receiving my testimony with Praise for God, it was turned into something ugly, which I never intended. To them, I was praising myself, and have turned many so-called Christians against me. I'm still in shock over their reaction, but I realize Satan is trying to destroy not only my testimony, but God's work. The battle is the Lord's, and He will fight for me and for His Word. God showed me Scripture that I call the "6 S's of Victory". Those "6 S's" have helped me through many battles!

> *"Ye shall not need to fight in this battle: set yourselves,*
> *stand ye still, and see the salvation of the Lord with you,*
> *O Judah and Jerusalem . . ."*
> —II CHRONICLES 20:17 KJV

The saddest part of this whole thing is the reaction of the church people. I thought the Church—Jesus Christ's Body on this earth—would rejoice at my victory. If this is the general attitude of the Christian Church in America, we need a complete renewal—a regeneration or rebirth! No wonder our country is in the condition it is in, with sin running rampant inside the Church as much as among the so-called "lost". "Born again" Christians should look and act completely different from the rest of the world. If we are to be called Christians, which means "little Christs", then we ought to be acting like Jesus. Every thought we think should measure up to Scripture before it comes out of our mouths.

> *"Jesus replied, 'If anyone loves me, he will obey my word . . .'*
> —JOHN 14:23 NET

Why aren't we obeying Him? Because we don't really love Him, we are playing Church, and trying to look good while our hearts and minds are still wicked.

It won't work, people! Examine your own heart!
Keep God's commandments of love and forgiveness in your heart at all times.

Another time I shared how God worked in my life when He helped me forgive my husband who left me and our three children. I am still in shock over the reactions of people when I gave my testimony about my husband leaving me. Two women were, once again, talking about forgiving their husbands for leaving them and having a child by their new wife. For one woman, it had been around sixteen–seventeen years. I'm not sure how long it had been for the other woman. They were talking about how long it took to forgive their ex-husbands, but that they had finally forgiven them. One woman said something like: "It's taken a long time to forgive him, but I have now. Nobody can forgive immediately. It takes everybody a long time." When I heard that, I knew I had to speak. So, I said, "I had the same thing happen to me that happened to both of you. My husband left me, married another woman, and had another child. I never hated him but forgave him, immediately." They both got furious at me! The younger one jumped up, gathered up her things, and yelled: "Stop condemning me!" I said, "I'm not condemning you. You are condemning yourself." She slammed the door when she left. I'm sure everyone in the classrooms all around heard the commotion.

At the same time all the attacks were coming at me, I saw a review about David Platt's book *Radical*. I borrowed the Pastor's copy and started reading. When I got to the part about the secret church, where people brought their Bibles and studied for hours—even the children were hungry to learn the Bible! I thought: "This is what I want to do in the *ASK* room on Sunday morning. This would be an alternative to regular Sunday School where people could read Scripture, ask questions, do word searches, use concordances, whatever it took, to discuss the meaning of what they read. No one person would give the answer to a question but all would use references and different translations to get the meaning of a verse. Questions could be freely asked and researched. I could envision real Spiritual growth in an open setting like this, but I had never been involved in one. It seemed to me to be God's answer to Prayer! God, direct me if this is what I should do! I need the Pastor's support and a way to advertise the *ASK* classroom to the church; also, I need to know about age limitations, and number of people to allow at one time.

One of the really interesting things about the Bible is that in Proverbs, there are thirty-one chapters, so one could be read each day of the month. It was November 14, 2017, and the Lord said:

"Read Proverbs for today."

So, that meant I needed to read Proverbs Chapter 14. As I was reading, verse 7 jumped out at me:

"Go from the presence of a foolish man, when thou
perceivest not in him the lips of knowledge."
—PROVERBS 14:7 KJV

God was teaching me that even though the stranger (angel's) visit was a significant milestone in my Christian walk with Him, not every person who calls themselves a Christian has the same knowledge or depth or relationship with the Lord. Our job is to just keep our own communication lines open to the Lord and let Him be God. We must keep obeying Him and loving Him. If we are not obeying Him, we are not loving Him!

Examine your own heart! It is imperative in 2020 that we, in the Church, repent and get our lives lined up with God's Word so we can live in victory over sin. They will: "know us by our love for one another" because we *will* be able to love one another by the power of The Holy Spirit.

" 'By this all will know that you are My disciples,
if you have love for one another.' "
—JOHN 13:35 NKJV

Clean and Forgiven

Telling your own personal sins to the world is not an easy thing to do...but God put it in my mind to admit the worse thing I ever did, and He would use it to save many other people from their sins:

> *"Is any sick among you? let him call for the elders of the church; and let them pray over him, anointing him with oil in the name of the Lord: And the prayer of faith shall save the sick, and the Lord shall raise him up; and if he have committed sins, they shall be forgiven him. Confess your faults one to another, and pray one for another, that ye may be healed. The effectual fervent prayer of a righteous man availeth much."*
> —JAMES 5:14–16 KJV

I have been guilty of sexual sin, and even though I know that millions of other people have been guilty of some type of sexual sin, it doesn't make me feel any better! When God said I should admit my worst sin, my immediate reaction was: "I don't want to do that." I know my sin was forgiven many years ago when I walked down a church aisle and rededicated my life to Jesus Christ. Since that time, I have drawn closer and closer to the Lord. However, there are people who know of my sin that may *not* be aware of my repentance and that since that time I have been learning how to live according to:

> *". . . and bringing into captivity every thought to the obedience of Christ..."*
> —II CORINTHIANS 10:5 KJV

My repentance cleansed me of my sin, but that particular scripture taught me that I could learn how to not fall back into the same sin, and even keep myself from all other sins:

> *"But if we walk in the light as He is in the light, we have fellowship with one another, and the blood of Jesus Christ His Son cleanses us from all sin.*
>
> *If we say that we have no sin, we deceive ourselves, and the truth is not in us.*
>
> *If we confess our sins, He is faithful and just to forgive us our sins and to cleanse us from all unrighteousness."*
> —I JOHN 1:7–9 NKJV

I love that little word *"all"*! The entire little book of I John tells us how we are to abide (live) in Jesus Christ, confess our sins, love others, and even overcome the world by believing:

> *"Who is it that overcomes the world?*
> *Only the one who believes that Jesus is the Son of God."*
> —I JOHN 5:5 NIV

There are repercussions from all sin, but we all *can* be free from constant guilt by confessing our sinfulness and rededicating our lives to Christ. My life has changed dramatically since that day in 1986 when I walked down that church aisle and told that group of Christians I had sinned and wanted to come back to Christ. It has been a long time now and God has done wonderful things in my life.

I know beyond a shadow of a doubt, *I am forgiven!*

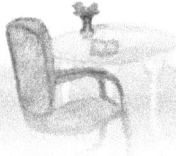

Diary Excerpts: 2017/2018

December 31, 2017:
God's Voice, Seeing Jesus, Temple

I t's 12:56 a.m. Dec. 31, New Year's Eve of 2017, and Jesus has been talking to me for at least 15–20 minutes to get up and write. I said I wish I felt more like writing, and He spoke to my spirit and told me that if I told myself I *did* feel like writing, I would! He also reminded me of the time years ago, when the children were still at home, and I was just learning how to hear God's voice and how to know what I was supposed to be doing. Very early one morning while I was still in bed, I was talking to the Lord, and praising and thanking Him for my new relationship with Him. I said, "Lord, what am I supposed to do today?" His very clear answer was, *"I can't direct you if you aren't up and moving."* I was so surprised I laughed out loud, and at once got up and got ready for whatever I thought He might direct me to do for the day. It also came to me, very clearly in my mind, that He can't help me write *Fortune and Paradise* if I don't have paper in front of me and a pen in my hand! God is so practical, but we try to spiritualize everything! We don't have to work at getting ready to do His will—just do it! We don't have to work up belief in every word in His Holy Book, we just need to *act* on what He says. Act, think, and talk healed, and we are! My Goodness! He just said that to me! Acting on our faith proves our belief in His Word!

> *"For as he thinks in his heart, so is he…"*
> —Proverbs 23:7 NKJV

> " 'Ask, and it will be given to you; seek, and you will find; knock,
> and it will be opened to you. For everyone who asks receives, and
> he who seeks finds, and to him who knocks it will be opened.' "
> —MATTHEW 7:7–8 NKJV

So, here I am writing about being on Mill Mountain, where I had been telling my story of how He healed me of cancer in 2009. I had just turned toward the deck of the overlook at the "World's Largest Man-Made Star" that looks down on our beautiful little city of Roanoke, Virginia. I had told the story of my miracle healing many times.

However, this time I looked up in the sky and I saw a vision of Jesus standing at the throne of God in a cloud of bright light. He was looking toward the East and turned slightly to His left to look down at me. He said to my spirit (not in an audible voice):

> *"Tell people I AM the same Jesus, healing people from
> My throne in Heaven as I did when I walked on the earth."*

It happened in such a flash of time, and I was so surprised, I started to wonder if I really saw Him. But it keeps coming back to my memory, so I am sure I really did see Jesus!

I am amazed every day of my life! I have been going to the Mountain every day when the weather isn't too frigid or pouring rain since December 2015. So often I meet people from all over the world. I just talked to someone from Tajikistan—it is country number ninety-one! I am keeping a record of all the different countries of the people I have talked to (just not how many people). I have told my cancer healing miracle many times and try to remember what Jesus said about the fact that He is still on His throne, and He is still healing people.

I am amazed that more people don't believe He is alive and very much involved in every part of our lives if we just let Him be. God, The Father, wants us to treat Him and to talk to Him as though He really *is* our Father; and Jesus wants us to know He really *is* alive and ready to heal and guide and protect and provide—and sometimes, He just wants to talk with us.

44

If we have been born again, as Jesus said in John 3:3 KJV, the third member of The Holy Trinity, The Holy Spirit, actually comes to live inside our body. Our human flesh actually becomes The Temple of God:

> *"What? know ye not that your body is the temple of the Holy Ghost which is in you, which ye have of God, and ye are not your own? For ye are bought with a price: therefore glorify God in your body, and in your spirit, which are God's."*
> —I CORINTHIANS 6:19–20 KJV

If we really believed these two verses, we would all act a whole lot better than we do! Everything we think, everything we say, and everything we do (including eating, and drinking, and working, and shopping, and sleeping, and playing, and reading, and watching tv, and texting, and on and on) should give God glory. Do you live like you belong to God? Do you talk to Him and listen to Him enough to know what you are supposed to be doing every minute of every day? And how do you spend your money? I could go on and on about that! Are you really living a Christian life, or just "playing Church"? Why doesn't Jesus heal everybody? Because we don't *believe* Him!

December 7, 2018:
Frozen Water, Life in 40s & 50s, Virgin

It is almost 3 p.m. on Monday, Dec. 7, 2018, and my water lines to the bathroom sink and shower suddenly stopped dripping water. I have left them open to drip for over a week now because the weather has been colder than I can remember. The kitchen pipes have been completely frozen for over a week, even though I had left them to drip, also. The water pipes travel under the floors of three rooms, so the water froze on the long trip. I've been carrying water from the bathroom for kitchen use. The weather report called for freezing rain, so I "wrapped up good" (like my mother used to say to me), got the flashlight and keys to the cellar door and went down to see what was going on. The freezing rain (not quite sleet) was coming down lightly. I unlocked the cellar door and discovered whoever the last person was who worked in my cellar didn't put the inside double-door back together, and my utility-size electric cord was lying in a puddle of water. I prayed for my attitude to stay loving and thankful for whatever work they did for me and decided it wasn't worth losing a friendship to say anything. If anyone helps me at all, that is worth much more to me than the neatness (or lack of) in doing the job.

This part of my writing is probably going to be more about Christian attitudes than the facts I will be telling about my life. My Daddy seldom complained about the way things were done, but Mama was just the opposite. One of her mottos was:

"If you are going to do something, do it right!"

. . . which meant do it her way or you'll have to do it over. I was so eager to learn about everything that doing things over didn't bother me. I was glad to learn how to do everything Daddy did with the animals, the gardening, and the tools; and everything Mama did with the cooking, the cleaning, the laundry (washing, hanging to dry, ironing, and folding), growing the flowers and doing some sewing. I learned to make and design doll clothes (and even hats) as soon as I could use a pair of scissors to cut the material and thread a needle to sew things together. By the time I was a teenager, I started making my own clothes. Some of them I even designed myself. I designed and made my own evening gown for my future husband's high school prom when I was sixteen and he was almost eighteen. It was beautiful, and my home economics teacher gave me a good grade and a lot of praise!

At that time in my life, I learned to cut my own hair. I could hold up a hand mirror in my left hand and look at the back of my head in the bathroom mirror and cut it evenly. I was very particular about how it looked. Short hair was in style and my hair waved easily, so I just wet it and pushed up waves in back and pin-curled one curl on each side at my ears and three or four pin-curls for my bangs. A couple of times Mama had a home perm put in my hair, but that always made it look frizzy and I didn't like it that way. In those days I had five different things to wear—one for each day of the week—but the poor girls had fewer than that. The richer girls wore new, in-style things, so I wasn't part of the in-crowd.

We never went hungry and we were always very clean because that's the way both of my parents were raised. Mama fussed sometimes because of having to make do with other peoples' old furniture; but once, when Daddy figured out how to make payments at Sears-Roebuck, he bought a maple dining room set with a long table that sat all six of us, a tall china cabinet, and a buffet. I have a clear memory of Daddy sitting at that table after meals were cleared away and taking a torn piece of a brown paper bag, a pencil, and a stack of envelopes (that I knew were bills) and he "figured and figured". That's what he called it when he was trying to decide how to "rob Peter to pay Paul". I didn't quite understand all that. I just knew he was really careful with his money and there never seemed to be quite enough. I have no idea how rich or poor we were. I just knew not to complain about anything because Daddy was trying so hard. I was still in high school when his eyesight went bad and he had to have surgery for holes in his retina. That was a difficult time. Mama had to go to work, so she learned how to be a Nurse's Aide and worked at the hospital every day.

I have always been so thankful for my childhood because I was raised in a church-going family. My Daddy got excited about all kinds of things. He planned all our trips and picnics and Sunday rides and going to the movies. Our movie fun times were in the downtown Roanoke theater at first. That cost a lot more. Then Daddy heard about the drive-in-movies where a whole carload could go for only $1 a car. We sat in the car and watched westerns with Gene Autry, Roy Rogers, Hopalong Cassidy, and others. He thought that was the greatest thing!—all six of us together in our car riding to a big field where we parked next to a speaker, which Daddy took off the stand and placed in the car.

We also saw some slapstick comedy, but I always got upset when things didn't "turn out right". I had such a powerful sense of doing the right thing because of being raised in a Christian home, with parents who considered a job Not Finished until it was done right, that I got emotionally distressed when the actors did "dumb" things. Other people laughed, but I had developed such an internal conviction of right and wrong that I hated those types of movies and still don't like comedy (or what the "world" calls comedy). I just don't believe it is funny when people don't have enough common sense to do the proper thing.

I don't think it is funny when people do things—that if *really* done in real life, would seriously hurt or even kill another person. I don't think it is funny to make fun of other people or call them names or be a bully. I don't think it is funny to say derogatory things against public officials and leaders, and certainly not the President of the United States. I don't think it is funny when men are made fun of in households seemingly run by women. I don't think it is funny when women degrade themselves by their manner, dress, or vulgar speech. I don't think it is funny when children are disrespectful to their parents, elders, or even their peers. I don't think it is funny when God, His Word, Christian people and/or principles are made fun of.

> *"Like a madman who throws firebrands, arrows, and death, Is the man who deceives his neighbor, And says, 'I was only joking!'"*
> —PROVERBS 26:18–19 NKJV

Yes, there are times (when I'm busy with the things of life) that He brings up memories from the past that I need to write about. These are just memories that, when I do sit down to write, He will bring to me again in a more orderly fashion, so I will know they are to be added to this narrative. Even though all throughout my life I have written poetry, long letters, and intense thoughts about different subjects, writing a book is vastly different. It requires an ordering of thoughts and sequencing of events; but also, attention to spelling, grammar, punctuation, congruency, purpose, and a sensible chain of events—plus a definitive ending to the general thought. I think the main point is how I became who I am, how I formed opinions about people, events, or activities, and what caused me to make the decisions I made.

I know that hearing about God was an early memory, and knowing He was watching me affected what I did. I knew I was supposed to be good and, to me, that meant: don't do or say anything to upset another person; don't be mean and hurt their feelings; don't take or break something that belongs to someone else; and don't say things that aren't true. I also remember, as I climbed as high as I could in every tree, that I felt closer to God when I was up high, looking at how big the world was, or feeling how warm the sun or how cooling the breeze. I thought about how good it felt to run and feel strong. Oh, how I wanted to learn about everything other people did. I was very aware of the differences in people and formed opinions of my own about good and bad, and it seemed I was able to just discern those things. I especially remember having strong feelings about wanting to be good.

I had a vague knowledge about the difference between boys and girls and knew early in life that those parts of my body were not to be uncovered, so I grew up very modest in my actions as well as my talk. I would not join in small groups of girls because I had an inner warning that they would say things that weren't nice. I don't know how I developed that knowledge at such an early age. Maybe it was something I learned at church. I just seemed to realize that some talk was inappropriate, so I became very shy, aloof, and quiet around other kids. I kept that aloofness for years and never shared my deepest thoughts with anyone. Of course, this affected all my relationships. It also kept me very innocent about sexual development, which had its good and bad effects. I remained a virgin in mind and body until I was married, which was good, but I never felt comfortable enough to ask questions to help understand my own body, much less the opposite sex. This lack of knowledge kept me a virgin (with a clean, innocent mind), but also vulnerable in a dangerous way because I didn't know the effect I could have on others. In fact, my innocence and lack of knowledge caused a lot of problems in my relationships.

Missing My Friend

God just reminded me of an incident that happened about two years ago with my friend (the one who got saved and born again into the family of God the same Sunday I rededicated my life to God in 1986). We had dated many years ago, and were even engaged for a brief period, but had always remained friends. Periodically, he would stop by my house to say hello and let me know he was still alive; but the last few times I saw him, his health was failing. He hired a woman to come live with him to cook, shop, clean, do laundry and drive for him because his eyesight had gotten so bad. One day I realized he hadn't stopped by for a long while, so I drove to his house, which was about a 40-minute drive. It had been years since I had been there. I knocked and knocked, but there was no answer and no vehicles in the driveway. After that I would call periodically, but no one ever answered. So, I just decided to not interfere in his life and went on with my own. One day, his face came to my mind. I had a strong feeling that something was wrong. I said to myself, "I wonder if he has the same phone number? Can I even remember it?" So, I went to what I thought was his number and looked it up. It was the right number, but instead of calling again, I decided to pray. I said: "Father God, I can't find my friend, so I'm going to leave it with You to help me find him. But right now, Father, I'm going up to the Star."

I put the phone book back in the drawer and left at once to go up to Mill Mountain. I parked my car in the lower lot near the Discovery Center and walked up the hill to the Star Overlook. I was there only a short time and didn't see anyone to talk to. So, on my way down the hill, instead of staying on the paved path, I decided to cut through the children's playground because it was a closer route to my car. All of a sudden, I heard a woman's voice calling, "Shirley! Shirley!" A tall young woman was running toward me. (I didn't recognize her at all.) She said, "Are you Shirley Morgan?" I said, "Yes!" (I still didn't know who she was.) She said, "I'm your friend's cousin." I would never have recognized her! She was a young teenager the last time I saw her; now she had two children. But the amazing thing was, it wasn't more than 30 minutes since I had told the Lord He was going to have to help me find my friend, and here was his cousin, right in front of me! She told me his health was worse and he had been put into a nursing home and was able to give me that name and address.

God is so involved in **every** part of our lives—if we just let Him be! He wants to be our Father and our God! He knew how important it was (to both of us) to not lose contact with one another!

Praise God!

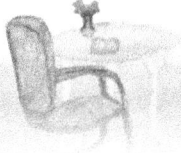

Diary Excerpts: June/July 2019

Men In Charge, Boys Important, Truth

A t one point, I was writing about how I turned out to be the kind of person I am. I decided early in life that I would rather be quiet, but fun and kind, rather than complaining. What I didn't say was that I believed in the old fashioned idea that men were in charge and that women should be under their authority.

When I married my first husband, it never occurred to me to discuss with him about how the money would be spent, where we would go and what we would do and how it was to be done. It never entered my mind to disagree, mainly because I was so young and knew very little about making important decisions about money and where to live, or how to buy a car, or even insurance. I knew about how to buy some food, but I didn't know a pork chop from a steak. I understood about budgeting money, if I knew what things cost, but he just made all the decisions without talking to me. I thought that was the way it was supposed to be. I never really heard Mama and Daddy discussing money.

I grew up being thankful for everything I had, even if it was secondhand. Even my clothes were all things from my cousins, or feed-sack dresses. On very rare occasions, I actually got a new dress, but all my play clothes were secondhand. I never owned a new bicycle. Daddy bought my brother a new bike so he could deliver newspapers when he was twelve years old. Then, when he was sixteen. Daddy bought him a car. (I think it was called an English Austin.) It made paper delivering a lot easier and faster. Daddy got my sister and me a job at the Kroger store as soon as we were sixteen.

I learned early that boys were more important than girls, but I never felt anger or jealousy. I just accepted it as the way things were.

It's a short explanation as to why I have been divorced four times. I didn't know I had any rights, and I was gullible enough to believe everything I was told. I decided I was going to always tell the truth or not say anything at all. I didn't know some people thought lying was okay to do if it kept you out of trouble.

4 Husbands, True Christian

I'm going to continue the explanation of how I became such a submissive woman because it shows how or why I ended up in four marriages that didn't work. My submissiveness to men was developed as a child to a loving Christian father. When I married my first husband, he declared he was going to be a Christian, and I believed him. I didn't know he was a party boy, addicted to alcohol and gambling, and he had no idea what it meant to live a Christian life. His Christian commitment didn't come until much later. He left when our son was baptized at age ten. My two daughters were already Christians. His exact words were: "I don't want to live in a house with a bunch of Christians."

Praise the Lord, he and his wife were active in church for many years before he passed away at age eighty-three. He had a very strong personality, and I was easily controlled and submissive. I just did what he said. My 2nd husband had a likable personality and things went well for a while; then I realized I was burdened with the strain of so much responsibility, and I became extremely disappointed. I found out my 3rd husband did not know how to treat women and was filled with distrust of them. He told me his mother locked him and his eight or nine siblings out of the house. My 4th husband was extremely intelligent, had a very high IQ and was raised in a Christian home; however, I was unaware of how much he was traumatized from Vietnam. I didn't know he was an addict, or that every addict is also a liar! They have to know how to be very good at lying to get their drugs. He was very talented in a lot of areas and a hard worker, going at everything like he was fighting the war again. There was never any peace; everything was done at top speed and with constant talk. I had to get away to stay sane myself! To him, lying was just another way to talk and get things done! He seemed to have no conscience about right and wrong and would steal without feeling guilty.

I couldn't believe I had been fooled *again*! I made up my mind never to marry again and not to believe anything a man said to me. If a man says, "I'm a Christian" I am going to watch his behavior first. My Mama said: "The Truth is in the pudding! Taste it and see!" This is why we need to encourage one another. It takes God's supernatural forgiving power to experience His peace in painful circumstances. We can't do it on our own. I just keep praying to God for His power to be able to continue to love and forgive!

Encourage One Another

The main reason my marriages failed was because of my belief that men were supposed to be in charge and women were supposed to submit. For me, that would mean agreeing to their law-breaking and their mistreatment of me. I couldn't live with either of those. And, I couldn't live without my strong beliefs about Bible reading, prayer, living my Christian principles, attending church every Sunday and Wednesday and revivals, and not lying, doing drugs, alcohol, dirty jokes, bad TV and on and on. It just didn't work for me, I was *too* Christian.

> *". . . endeavoring to keep the unity of the Spirit*
> *in the bond of peace."*
> —EPHESIANS 4:3 NKJV

> *"Therefore comfort each other and edify one another,*
> *just as you also are doing."*
> —I THESSALONIANS 5:11 NKJV

> *". . . but exhorting one another, and so much the more as*
> *you see the Day approaching."*
> —HEBREWS 10: 25 NKJV

> *"Therefore, as we have opportunity, let us do good to all,*
> *especially to those who are of the household of faith."*
> —GALATIANS 6:10 NKJV

Adultery

I didn't always do everything right. I was a sinner, just like the Bible says in Romans:

". . . for all have sinned and fall short of the glory of God,"
—ROMANS 3:23 NKJV

I was a virgin when I first married and I didn't have sex before marriage to my 2nd, 3rd, or 4th husbands; but I did commit adultery. This sounds absolutely stupid to say, but I didn't have any idea what to do with the married men who wanted to have sex with me. I was so used to doing what men demanded, that I just caved in. (I guess you could call it that.) I didn't like that situation at all. I argued against it and tried to not get involved, but they wouldn't leave me alone. I didn't have a strong enough personality to fight back, but I did try! I didn't like kidding and I never did learn how to just lie! So, I guess I mixed up the truth some. I hated it and eventually got brave enough to just say "No!" and keep on saying "No!" The people who don't commit adultery cannot condemn those who do, because the Bible says—Jesus, Himself, said:

" 'But I say to you that whoever looks at a woman to lust for her has already committed adultery with her in his heart.' "
—MATTHEW 5:28 NKJV

In the book of Matthew 5:1 NKJV where it says:

(Jesus) *". . . He went up on a mountain . . ."*

to Matthew 8:1 NKJV where it says:

(Jesus) *". . . He had come down from the mountain . . ."*

He taught about specific sins of the flesh. All sin starts in the minds of people; therefore, we are all guilty before God and cannot condemn another person because you think their sin is worse than your own. The Gift that Jesus brought to this earth, is Himself, as the Perfect Sacrifice, to pay for every sin ever conceived in the mind of every person who has ever lived. It is of extreme importance that we do not judge and condemn others as worse than ourselves, because that attitude is also sinful. I believe it is the biggest problem in the Body of Christ or The Church. When you look at another person and call them self-righteous, you have immediately become self-righteous to set yourself up above the person you condemn. Jesus has paid for my sin, and I accept His payment with great Joy! Now I pass on this love and forgiveness to others, which is our mission as Christians—not to judge and condemn, but to set them free! It is why I am writing my story.

Purpose in Writing Sins, Simple Life

God had to tell me again today to put a piece of paper in front of me and a pen in my hand, and He would tell me what to write. So, here I am again, saying one more time, why I am writing my sins down in my *Fortune and Paradise* book. Certainly not for money! Money has never been a driving force in my life. I guess, to the people who do have money as their driving force, that statement sounds ridiculous. Even as a child, I didn't think about being rich when I grew up. I looked at the people in my life who had more money, a more beautiful house, filled with more things, much better cars, more beautiful clothes, and went on perfect vacations, and I couldn't see that they were any happier than me. I loved my life on our little farm and being free to roam on all the neighbors' farms that included creeks and small mountains, ponds to swim or fish in, and beautiful views from the tree-tops I climbed.

We always knew that when Daddy came home from his railroad job, he would work a little in the garden, or build something, milk the cows, and strain the milk through cheese cloth and put it in the refrigerator before we sat down to eat the supper Mama had cooked. Then, there were dishes to wash and put away, laundry to bring in and fold or put in the ironing basket, homework to finish, bath and bedtime. It was a very simple life.

There was no such thing as television, and we couldn't afford a telephone. If we had something really important that required a telephone, we went down the path to Grandma's house. (I don't know why we never called it Papa's house.) He was always sitting in his chair in the "little room", which is what Papa's room next to the kitchen was called. Papa's war injury (that no one talked about) prevented him from doing any work.

He could sit there and watch everything Grandma did in the kitchen. I seldom saw her anyplace besides the kitchen making buttermilk and butter, canning fruits and vegetables, making pickles, and washing dishes. A few times I saw her in the wash house (which was a few steps from the back porch door) where she did the family laundry and hung the wash on clothes lines between the wash house and the big shed that was a type of garage for the tractors and farm equipment. The only time I saw Grandma sit down was when she was squeezing milk from the butter she had taken from the churn. After she squeezed all the milk out, she put ice cubes in the butter to get it cold, and with her hands and fingers pressed it into the wooden form to make a pound of butter with all flat, smooth sides and nice square corners. She kept the butter cold with the ice cubes so that when she pushed the formed butter out, it was perfect. It had to go directly into the ice-box on the kitchen porch to keep it cold and preserved from the heat of summer days or the fires that were heating the house in winter.

Life seemed so safe, simple, and secure to me during those early years. The only real problem I had was my own mother's treatment of me. Some things can't be explained.

Physical Growth, Dirty Jokes, Capturing Thoughts

My two sisters' bodies were similar. They were taller and what Mama called long-waisted with longer arms and legs and wore much smaller bras. Mama called me short-waisted, and I just kept developing. I began to get a lot of attention from boys and even some girls made comments. I just stayed quiet because I never talked about what I considered to be embarrassing subjects or listened to dirty jokes.

In one of the offices where I was the receptionist, I had to greet everyone and help them get to the correct office. I had to tell one of the salesmen early in our acquaintance not to use vulgar talk around me or tell dirty jokes. One day, while all the other employees were gone, he came up to my desk and started talking like he was telling a story about a friend of his. It was actually a very lewd joke, but I didn't realize it until he got to the punch line, which, to me, was not funny. I got angry and said: "I told you not to tell me dirty jokes." His response was: "You're a drip" (which, way back in that time, was considered an insult). I think I said: "Thank you. Don't do that again!"

I was very strong in my Christian witness at that time; but I'm sorry to say that another man was able to tear down my wall of resistance. I understand completely how Christians can be led into sin because it happened to me. It took a long time and a lot of prayer and determination, but I was finally able to build up my wall of resistance; and now in 2019, I can say I have lived a celibate life, even in my thinking, for over twenty-three years. Jesus said:

> " 'But I say to you that whoever looks at a woman to lust for her has already committed adultery with her in his heart.' "
> —MATTHEW 5:28 NKJV

When I went to India, that angel (with no face) sat down beside me in that huge ballroom, and told me to learn to live by II Corinthians 10:5:

> ". . . bringing every thought into captivity to the obedience of Christ . . ."
> —II CORINTHIANS 10:5 NKJV:

My life completely changed! I began to pay close attention to every thought in my head and to cast it out if it was sinful in the least degree. I lived like that for years. It has taken all the willpower I could summon to say: "I cast out that thought, in Jesus' Name!" or "Lord, take away that wicked thought!" and after all these years, it has become easier and easier to get rid of every evil thought that Satan tries to put in my mind! I literally say: "You get away from me, devil! I'm not having that thought in my mind!" and it goes away. ***Praise God!***

Ask God Who to Marry

Lord, I have my paper and pen in hand. Where do you want me to go today with my story? *I am praying for this entire project to save souls* (especially of other women who have had a difficult time with men in their lives). I guess my handsome, fun, funny, hard-working, honest, Christian father set too high of a standard of behavior for any of my husbands to match. I'm not blaming them for the failure of my marriages; I blame myself for marrying them in the first place. The main reason for my big mistakes in judgment was that I had no idea what love between a man and a woman was supposed to look like, feel like, or act like.

If I can help just one young girl not do what I did, this book will be a success!

- Don't marry a person who does not pray with you; if you are a dedicated Christian yourself, you need a husband who loves the Lord more than he loves you!
- Don't expect him to change for the better after you are married—even though he might! If he (or you) makes decisions without prayer, you are headed for trouble!
- Develop a personal relationship with the Lord. Learn to talk to Him and learn to listen to Him:

"Your word is a lamp to my feet And a light to my path."
—PSALM 119:105 NKJV

If you think I'm being too harsh or judgmental, you have no idea what living with people who are into parties, gambling, alcohol, drugs, and who generally do not put God first is like! Don't try it! Needless to say, the Christians I married didn't know what it meant to live the Christian life.

I am sorry for my share in the failure of each of my marriages, and the failure to make prayer a crucial element of its success. I realize more and more every day how important it is to pray and seek the face of the Lord and His answers to all the questions of life. When I struggle or get overwhelmed with the weight of the responsibility and consequences of making every decision as a single person, I remember I am not alone. You promised, Lord, You would be my husband:

"For thy Maker is thine husband; the Lord of hosts is his name; and thy Redeemer the Holy One of Israel; The God of the whole earth shall he be called."
—ISAIAH 54:5 KJV

Knowing Jesus, Christianity

I t is a beautiful day—even though it is supposed to get very warm and humid. I'm so glad, Lord, that You are my God and that You sent Jesus, Your only begotten Son, to this earth to die on that cross in Jerusalem so many years ago to pay the debt of my sin. I'm very thankful I had a Christian home to grow up in, and that my best memories and most important lessons about life were learned in my family and my church. I was born in 1936, so by the time of WWII I was old enough to realize war is a serious thing. People get killed, and living in fear of bombs hitting your house in the middle of the night is scary to a young child. I'm so glad, since I was raised in a church-going family, that I believe in Heaven after death for all who believe Jesus is God's Son, and that His death paid for all my sins so I could go to Heaven when I die. It is an amazing thing for a six to eight year old child to not fear death because they know Jesus. My belief was real—not just a "story" I heard at church. I talked to God before I was old enough to go to school because I knew He was real! I liked being a Christian and tried to be obedient to the rules at home and school and made an extra effort to be nice to other children—especially if I could tell they were poorer than me. I suppose some adults think children don't understand Christianity. Of course I didn't understand everything; but I did understand the basics, and that belief kept me from a lot of bad choices I could have made—even though I did make some bad choices. I always eventually talked to God about everything, and I knew I was forgiven!

The main thing Christianity taught me had to do with my own honesty and my caring for other people, especially if they seemed to be poor or not very pretty, or when other richer, smarter kids weren't nice to them. I made an effort, even in the 1st grade, to be friendly to outcasts. My own life is proof that children understand social acceptance and shunning. The decision I made in the 1st grade to be friends with the only Syrian girl in our class, was the beginning of my training, and I have always believed God arranged the whole thing for my development as a Christian! I've never had a racist thought, or judged people because of their skin color or type of clothes. I developed a real sense of compassion for people at a young age. I was eight years old when I was baptized, and I took my commitment to Jesus very seriously.

And that's why I want everyone to know Jesus!

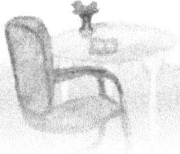

"Black" and "White" Memories

Introduction

My memories of growing up in a rural, middle-class, white neighborhood include some disturbing incidents that helped shape the way I think about racial issues. Even with all the advances our country has made toward equality for all races, cultures and religions, there are a lot of memories that need healing. There was a Black community not far away, so there was some interaction from time to time as my family engaged in daily life. One reason I'm writing these memories is to let Black people know that not all prejudices of previous generations will be accepted by all future generations, and that some of us white people saw the ugliness of prejudice as something to avoid. Another reason for my writing is to present an opportunity for self-examination by whites who "caught" prejudice from family, friends, and neighbors without considering the impact on their own lives and even the future of our country and world. Wars are fought, people killed, communities wiped out, and lives made miserable on all sides, by the simple refusal to see all people as people. This earth is big enough and rich enough in resources and possibilities for all of us to have enough. Our individual pride and selfishness are the cause of our misery, and we can't complain about someone else if we are thinking the same way they are. We are all made in the image of God.

> *"So God created man in His own image . . ."*
> —GENESIS 1:27 NKJV

> *"If someone says, "I love God," and hates his brother, he is a liar; for he who does not love his brother whom he has seen, how can he love God whom he has not seen? And this commandment we have from Him: that he who loves God must love his brother also."*
> —I JOHN 4:20–21 NKJV

I have some vivid memories of my childhood that helped form who I have become. I wouldn't call some of them good memories, but they are so valuable that I wouldn't take anything for them. The following is a series of events that strongly influenced my development as a loving, caring person, very aware of other people around me with a knowledge of right and wrong way beyond my years. My first memory of meeting a Black person was on my first bus ride.

My First Bus Ride

I was a skinny little girl with almost black hair and brown eyes, always jumping around and always asking questions. I held tightly to my Daddy's hand as the big bus came into sight, so excited about going on my first bus ride. We lived in Green Ridge (what we called the country) close to the Blue Ridge Mountains. Grandma and Papa (Daddy's mother and father) had a farm in a settlement of Dunkard people. Daddy and one of his brothers built their houses and had small gardens on their own acreage while they helped with the work on the main farm. They both also worked for the railroad in what was called the shops. Grandma and Papa had an automobile that everyone shared, so it helped our area a great deal as this was before bus service became available. When service did become available, people who rode the bus regularly were able to buy a pass at a lower price. Daddy and his brother were the type of people who loaned their passes to other family members when they weren't using them.

I remember how safe I felt with my Daddy when the bus stopped, and the door opened, and I was lifted to the first step. Daddy was tall and very handsome, I thought, like the men in the cowboy movies he took us to see sometimes. I looked all around the inside of the bus: at the driver, at a woman on the seat behind the driver, and at a lot of empty seats. Daddy was trying to get on and show his passes for our ride while I just stood there in the way, taking it all in—the sound of the engine, the smell of the bus, and all the windows. Then, when Daddy tried to guide me to one of the front seats, I spotted the big, long seat across the whole back of the bus, and said, "I want to sit on that back seat!" It looked like the most fun place to me! I'm sure Daddy had difficulty thinking of what to say. He never was much of a talker, but he said something like: "You can't sit there. That's for those people already there. You have to sit up front." I saw several people sitting there, staring at me, with solemn, brown faces and no smiles. They didn't act like the back seat was fun at all!

"Colored"

One time, while we were waiting for our train to arrive so we could start our trip, I walked all around the inside of the train station looking at everything. I noticed two water fountains: one said "White" and the other one said "Colored". I asked Daddy why there were two water fountains with "White" and "Colored" signs on them. Daddy just said that colored people couldn't drink from the same fountain as white people did. I remember thinking how strange that was.

Another clear memory was when Mama and I went to a Five and Dime store. At lunch time, we sat at a counter on high stools. I saw a colored man come in and talk to a waitress behind the counter. She prepared a hot dog and put it in a brown paper bag and handed it to him at the cash register. He gave her some money and left. I said, "Mama, where is he going to eat?" She said, "He's going outside." I said, "He can sit by me. Nobody is sitting on this stool," and I pointed to the stool next to me. Mama said, "He can't eat in here." I worried about that a long time before I finally realized it was because he was colored. I thought that was not very nice of white people! I was probably five or six years old.

Just Not "White"

In the first grade of school, there was one little girl named Mary who had darker skin than the rest of us. She was from Syria. One day she came to me crying because the other kids were calling her a bad name. I tried to say things to make her feel better, but after a short period of time, she didn't come to school there anymore. I wondered all my life why she chose me to be her friend! I've always considered that incident to be a great compliment to me and a special treasure to my heart. I finally realized she liked me as a friend because I, also, had almost black hair and very dark brown eyes, and I was the only child who talked to her. Sad!

My mother had a sister named Margaret who married a Syrian man and they had three children named Johnny, Janice, and Jacqueline. They came to visit us one time and Daddy took us all to an amusement park for an outing. It was full of different rides: bumper cars, ferris wheel, roller coaster, horse carousel, train, and little airplanes, and there was a fun house and an arcade area. The ticket man at the gate wouldn't let us in because my cousins' skin was darker than ours! My Daddy was so embarrassed, and everyone was so terribly upset! How do you explain that to children? I grew up having a tender heart toward people. I consider that sensitivity to others to be a special gift from God.

Clean Feet

I was too little to know why Mama was gone (later I learned she had been in the hospital) and why a colored woman was in our house taking care of us. I just knew Mama was sick. I never cried for her because I was treated so well by this stranger—a strong, young, dark-skinned woman. One memory stands out because of the impact it made on me physically and emotionally.

I had already had my bath and was in my pajamas. At bedtime, this woman picked me up and held my feet in the bathroom sink while she washed and dried them. I was so surprised! I remember asking her why she was washing my feet, "So you won't be putting dirty feet in a clean bed" was her answer. Then, I was even more surprised when she carried me up the steep, narrow staircase leading to the two upstairs bedrooms and put me in the bunk bed below my older sister's bed. This is the only memory I have of being held or carried during my entire childhood, except for one incident when I was around two years old. Our family had been out late one night and when we got home, I was so sleepy I headed for a big stuffed chair, climbed up and got on my knees with my face down in the soft cushion, where I went right back to sleep. I'm pretty sure it was my Daddy who took off my coat and hat and shoes and put me to bed.

I have no memory of anyone else ever picking me up or even hugging me. I was never told I was loved, never kissed goodnight, never told I was pretty, or that I could do anything well—except when I was big enough to clean house, the bathroom was my responsibility because I "cleaned it better than my older sister." I was very proud of that!

The memory of that colored woman holding me and carrying me was one bright spot of feeling cared for in a childhood devoid of any expression of love or any touching of any kind. I'm not criticizing or judging, just stating facts the way they were. Daddy was from a large family. Mama's mother died when Mama was eight and her father died when she was fifteen. It made an enormous impact on her life. But it was this young, caring colored woman who made such an impression on my heart that I became especially sensitive to any derogatory talk (particularly the N-word—I hated that word and never used it). She showed me what life could be by showing true caring for a little white girl.

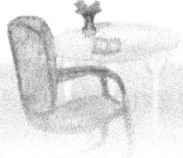

Little Girl Growing Up

I always felt different because I didn't have seven teeth most people have. There were big gaps between my teeth, and I considered myself ugly. In high school I talked and laughed with my hand over my mouth for a long time because I was so embarrassed about how I looked. I also had to wear glasses beginning in the third grade. I was very shy and quiet and not part of the in-crowd. I began to look a little prettier as I became a teenager, but I was still not one of the popular girls. I had a small group of particularly good friends, so it wasn't all bad. I never joined a sorority. I was invited to join one; but Daddy said if they met on Sunday, I couldn't join, so I didn't. Church was more important to me, anyway, and I agreed with Daddy.

I was very close to God as a small child, even before I could read. I remember talking to God one night, standing outside our basement door and looking up at the sky that was covered with stars. I said, "God, how can You see me from way up there? I'm so little and there are so many people in the world!"

I was reared in church. We were there every Sunday—morning and evening—for preaching and Sunday School and Baptist Training Union. All our family activities were either with church people or Daddy's big family. Mama was orphaned as a child, and we were too far away from her big, scattered family in West Virginia and Pennsylvania to know them very well. I had God in my heart before I could read or really understand very much about Jesus. However, when my older sister went down the church aisle to be saved, I followed her because that was what I wanted, too! I was eight years old. I remember clearly, thinking to myself as I was getting into the car to go home: "Now, I'll be a good girl."

Well, I wasn't a bad girl to begin with but somehow Mama seemed to think so, and I got a lot of whippings that I didn't understand. I think Mama must have been mistreated by different people she had to live with and maybe she thought she was doing the right thing. I don't think I ever deliberately did bad things like lying, or stealing, or cheating, and I didn't join groups of girls because I didn't talk about boys. I grew up pretty much alone—except for playing with my siblings and cousins. I spent a lot of time climbing the big sycamore trees in our yard and playing with my brother on the mountain ridge around our farm, or in the several little creeks in the area. I talked to God a lot while I played, and I knew I never wanted to be mean to other people or cheat at school, and I didn't like going to parties at all! I didn't want to hear what I called bad things, so I was friends only with other girls that I knew were Christians. It probably sounds strange (or even unbelievable) that I was a virgin when I got married at 18. I decided early on, as soon as I understood what virgin meant, that I was going to be one! I never listened to dirty jokes in my whole life! I would just get up and leave whatever group of people I was in if someone even started to tell jokes, and I never listened to gossip or repeated anything I accidentally heard. God was very important to me from a young age, and I wanted to be good more than popular.

Daddy helped my older sister and me get jobs at the Kroger store in Salem as soon as we were sixteen years old. We had to work weekends, so I didn't get to go to the football games on Friday night like most of the other kids did. The captain of the football team asked me for a date one Saturday night. We went to a drive-in movie and then got a cola after the movie. I was so shy I didn't talk, so he never asked me again. I liked him and knew he was a Christian, but I was very immature and knew nothing about football. I was so uncomfortable I was glad he didn't ask me out again. It was different when I met my future husband. I was always comfortable around him. He did all the talking and I just listened and sometimes asked a question or made a comment, but I felt relaxed and not like I had to be on my guard. We dated for two years while I was still in high school.

Childhood Memories

After living eighty-four years, if there is just one thing I would want everyone in the whole world to know, it is that the great Creator God loves His Creation.

He loves the heavens and this earth and sun and moon and all the creatures on this earth. But most of all, He loves the people He made to be His children, so He can love us the way a father loves his children— just ever so much more and deeper than an earthly father. He *wants* to be called Father!

The great Creator of *all* the universe, with *all* knowledge, *all* wisdom and *all* power, who lives in *all* holiness and *all* purity and *all* love beyond *all* description wants to be known as Father! That is amazing beyond words!

We know this because when Jesus' disciples asked Him to teach them how to pray like He prayed, His answer was:

> " 'After this manner therefore pray ye:
> Our Father which art in heaven,
> Hallowed be thy name.
> Thy kingdom come,
> Thy will be done in earth,
> as it is in heaven.
> Give us this day our daily bread.
> And forgive us our debts,
> as we forgive our debtors.
> And lead us not into temptation,
> but deliver us from evil:
> For thine is the kingdom,
> and the power, and the glory, for ever. Amen.' "
> —MATTHEW 6:9–13 KJV

I learned this prayer when I was a child in church every Sunday, without fail, unless I was sick! But it didn't occur to me until much later in life (after I became a parent myself) that God wanted my love in response to His love for me!

". . . God is love."
—I JOHN 4:8 NKJV

If you love someone, you naturally want a relationship with them. You want to spend time with them, and you want to share life with them. That is what God wants from us. He wants to share life with us! That means we have to seek Him out, talk to Him, and talk about Him with others; and because He is God, He wants us to worship Him with His other children. That is the reason we have church services. God gets great pleasure in His family getting together to pray, sing, read His Book, and try helping each other, just like earthly parents want to see their children showing love to each other. Sometimes He has to correct our behavior—and often it takes a problem before His children come to Him for help.

I have good memories of my earthly father because I felt loved. He wasn't the kind of man who was comfortable talking about love, or any emotional subject. I remember the day he came home from his job on the railroad and his first words were: *"The Japanese bombed Pearl Harbor."* That's all I remember of that conversation, and the only word I understood was bombed. I didn't know who the Japanese were, and I had no idea what Pearl Harbor was. Things in our life changed drastically that day. There was no television, and Mama only listened to music, or the *Arthur Godfrey* program, or *The Breakfast Club with Don McNeill* on the radio. I remember we suddenly couldn't have all the sugar we wanted, and our food had to be divided and shared equally. That was a very good lesson that stuck with me the rest of my life. We also had blackout practice when Mama and Daddy covered all our windows with blankets at night so no lights could be seen from outside. My grandfather, Papa Morgan, was the neighborhood watchman and he had to go to every house to make sure no lights could be seen, so we wouldn't be bombed by the enemy.

When we went to the movie theater, we saw news reels of the war. I still have terrible childhood memories of watching armed soldiers pushing great numbers of men, women, and children onto train boxcars to be taken to German camps where they were put to death in gas chambers. I was too young to understand what all that meant. I just remember the pictures and some of the words I heard like: "Jews killed" and "Hitler" and all the adults became very serious about everything. My brother and I played "war" instead of "cowboys and Indians," and the pictures we drew changed from copying the comics to drawing swastikas and airplanes dropping bombs. We didn't have any idea what the swastika was; we just liked drawing it, so we put it on everything. The adults never corrected us about that. I guess they didn't want to have to explain what it meant; and as long as we didn't know, it wouldn't hurt anything. I loved going to the movies, but I hated the news reels of the war because it scared me.

I remember when Daddy's youngest brother, Ralph, dressed in his army uniform, came out of Grandma's back door, and hugged her goodbye. He never came back again. Daddy was never drafted into the army. I was glad he never had to go.

After the war was over, life became less scary, Daddy got back his fun personality and the talk of war didn't come up again until I was a teenager working my first job as a cashier in a Kroger store, along with my older sister. Daddy came earlier than usual to pick us up to go home. He told us his oldest sister's oldest son (my cousin), was killed in Korea. He left behind his wife (pregnant with their daughter), two little boys, two brothers and two sisters, his parents and grandparents, and the rest of a huge hurting family: aunts, uncles, and cousins. War leaves uncountable scars.

For the most part, my childhood was simple and pleasant. My two sisters, my brother and I played together, and on weekends we played with our city cousins who came to visit Grandma and Papa. Grandma's house was about two-tenths of a mile away, with a well-worn path and tractor trail in-between. Daddy's second oldest brother lived next to Grandma and Papa's house, with an open field in between. He and his wife had two boys who were much too young to play with us.

Eventually, my older sister and I were their babysitters when our aunt and uncle went out or were working.

Mama's people lived in West Virginia and Pennsylvania. We lost track of them after high school. However, my most vivid childhood memories were of Daddy and me together. I followed him around all the time to see what he was doing and to help him in any way I could, so I could learn to do what he did. I was (what was called then) a tom-boy. I loved everything Daddy did because I loved him and wanted to do what he was doing. I was his go-getter when he needed a special tool or a certain nail size and his holder, which meant I had to hold on tight when he was building a fence, or nailing a board, or using a long measuring tape. Daddy figured on a flattened, brown paper bag and always planned everything on paper before he built it. I also learned to work the hay-rake while he drove the tractor to rake the hay into long piles. I was so skinny and small that I had to put my entire weight on the handle to release the forks of the hay-rake as Daddy drove through the hay field. So, I became Daddy's "second boy". I could run faster and climb a tree higher than my brother or either sister, and I was strong for my size; but the best part was that I liked everything I did, so it was enjoyable for Daddy to have me around.

When I got big enough to feed and care for the chickens, rabbits, and pigs, and even put the cow feed in the trough, I was the one behind Daddy's every step. I never complained about what I had to do. Daddy was so patient to explain exactly how to do each chore. I was the one who had to take items back and forth to Grandma's house or go to the orchard and pick some apples off the ground for Mama to cook. My instructions were to not pick apples off the tree. Pick up the good ones—with no rotten places—off the ground. It was "take this to Grandma's" and "run down to Grandma's and get that." I never complained because I loved the running part! I was such a tom-boy that I spent a lot of time climbing the sycamore trees on our property. I never had a new bike. There was an old junk pile at Grandma's, and my brother and I found enough pieces to make a bike for me. (I think my brother actually got a new bike—maybe because he had a job delivering newspapers every day on a very long country route.) I got to use my bike to help him sometimes.

One very good thing about my childhood that has helped me get through life without a lot of complaining, was to be thankful for everything I had, and to learn as much as I could about how to do everything I did. I didn't know I was preparing for adulthood; but the lessons of discipline and determination that I learned as a child have made my adult life so much easier. My mother and father both worked, even when they were tired, to get whatever job done. Mama dealt with recurring migraine headaches and other health problems, and Daddy started getting sick and lost a great deal of his eyesight in his 40's and was disabled—unable to work. Mama had to learn how to be a Nurse's Aide at the hospital and worked until retirement. Sometime after that she moved to a retirement community and stayed there for as long as she felt able. Then she decided to go to a nursing home where she lived for fifteen years before passing away at ninety-three. Daddy died before he was sixty. What I learned from both of them is priceless: *Do what you have to do—and do it right—the first time!*

They were both organized, disciplined and very dependable as employees and taught those values to us kids. Mama complained all the time but kept on going. Daddy seldom complained; so, when he did, we all knew he felt really bad. I could feel my Daddy's love for me, but I never felt love from my mother until the very end of her life, when she finally realized that she could depend on me for whatever she needed.

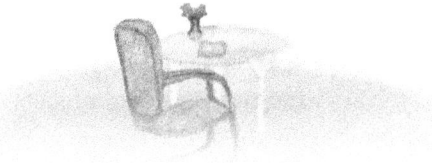

Child to Woman
First Marriage

I have written in detail about the innocence of my childhood that, for years, carried over into my marriage. My early years had formed an attitude about men and women or, I should say, myself as a woman, which affected everything I thought and did. My strong Christian Daddy showed me how life should be: Daddy works a job. Daddy does the farm work, and the carpentry work on the house. Daddy makes the decisions about going to church every Sunday, morning and evening, and every Wednesday night to prayer meeting. Daddy handles the money, pays the bills, buys the groceries, and all other things. Daddy plans our fun activities such as Sunday drives, picnics, and trips to see Mama's family. Mama takes care of our personal needs: cleanliness, clothes, food, house, flowers, and doctor visits. I guess you could say I had a "picture perfect / story-book" idea about marriage, so I never did want to work and leave my children, but I was forced to.

After eighteen years of marriage, my husband left, and I got a second job delivering newspapers. I soon met a Christian man, much younger than me, and we married after a very short courtship. I thought God put him in my life to take the place of my children's father and be my other half and that we would have a Christian home and things would be wonderful. The negative side of my attitude about men and women is that, since I viewed men as being in charge, I had not learned how to speak up for myself, express my opinion about anything or even have a personal desire to succeed at anything—except being a wife and mother. Of course, that made me a very boring person to be around.

I even seemed boring to myself when I was around other people. I had an intense desire to learn about all kinds of things and read books about "great and famous" people's lives. I asked questions about politics and business, but seldom understood the answers I was given. I didn't want to talk to people because I felt so inadequate; however, I did continue my search for knowledge and listened to other people talk. Of course, I grew up without television, so when I came home from France, it was a novelty and I watched it a lot while we were living in a tiny shack with two babies and an outdoor johnny house and cows in the yard on a neighbor's land next to my childhood home.

Our first house purchase was a four-room cottage with an inside bath and a small enclosed back porch where we eventually put an electric washing machine. My husband didn't like taking the kids to the laundromat and I didn't drive. We only had one car and I was too scared to do things in the world by myself. He got a job for me as a waitress at night after he got off from work, so he could keep the babies. I hated having to work in public and talk to strangers and felt so really dumb about everything. I finally learned how to be a really good waitress, and the clientele got used to me and I was more relaxed and even made tips. But I hated being away from home and my babies. The biggest problem was learning how to deal with the public, especially men who flirted with me, which brings on an entirely new and difficult problem I had to learn how to deal with. That's another chapter in my life!

No one would understand the change in my heart unless they knew the whole story. No one has ever asked, so I never told anyone what really happened to me inside my heart and why I ended up divorced so many times. I guess from the outside looking in at me, I just looked like a sinful woman going from man to man, but the *inside* story is much deeper and more painful than that. I was a child when I married at 18 and it took years to develop into womanhood. I will try to describe my childhood without placing blame or judging others, but all I know is what was in my own mind.

I had a very strong sense of right and wrong from as far back as I can remember. I knew I wanted to be good—that I never wanted to hurt anyone—but I also didn't want to see anyone else get hurt. So, when I saw someone being hurt, I would take their side. I actually had a short fight with another girl in elementary school because she was picking on someone else, and I pulled her off and made her stop.

I got really upset with myself for fighting, but a bunch of the other kids called me "the champ" and held my arms up like a winner. That didn't make me feel good, though. I put my head down on my desk; I was so ashamed of fighting—even if I did help someone who was being bullied. I knew I didn't fit in with the popular, rich girls, but I also didn't fit with the poor girls who had dirty hair or old-looking clothes. Mama made sure we were always clean and neat and had our hair clean and curled or combed. I made really good grades, but not always straight A's like my older sister.

Another reason I didn't feel like I fit in was because I wore glasses, and that wasn't cool like it is now. And then the teachers didn't pick me for the special school programs. They always picked the girls who wore new, store-bought clothes—not homemade or hand-me-downs. I made up my mind very early in elementary school to stay away from groups of girls who were the popular ones. I knew when they got in groups and giggled and whispered, they were either talking about boys or things that might embarrass me, so I stayed away. I used to run as hard as I could to the very back of the playground and climb a small bank where there were a few bushes and sit and just look around until it was time to go back to class. No one ever fussed at me for that, and I was able to avoid all that embarrassing girl talk.

Needless to say, I grew up knowing nothing about my own body or boys' bodies, and my mind and body stayed pure for a long time. I never listened to a dirty joke in my life. I just got up and left if people started telling jokes. I didn't want my mind to be dirty. I went all the way through high school with the same attitude to be nice to people, to not have bad thoughts, or listen to what I considered to be gossip or mean talk about others. I reached out some, especially to those I could tell were Christian, specifically three girls. I joined the Latin Club and was the Correspondence Secretary, and during my senior year I was the Circulation Manager for the yearbook, so I came out of my shy self a little bit.

I had only three or four dates before I started dating my future husband. I was quiet and shy, and not much fun; but he and I seemed to fit together, and we just felt comfortable, not strained. I was still very quiet and just let him decide where we went on dates. I was coming out of my backwardness (as Mama called it) and I became more active in conversations at school and in school activities. I was still very Christian in all my behavior and determined to not have sex before marriage. I am so glad I stuck by my beliefs! When he got his orders to be stationed in France, he asked me if I would wait for him. He told me stories of other guys who had gotten "Dear John" letters where their girlfriends or even some wives wrote to break up their relationship. I was very honest in my answer: "Two years is a long time. I don't know what will happen." Then he said, "Don't you love me?" He never told me he loved me—ever! I guess those words were too difficult for him to say. I answered, "Yes!" because I really felt that I did, even though I grew up without ever hearing "I love you" from my parents, or anyone else. I also don't recall anyone ever holding me on their lap or hugging me or showing me any evidence of that kind of physical love, so I really had no idea what love was. I just knew I felt really at ease with my future husband, and I liked the way he looked, and admired his easy-going, friendly personality and his intelligence. I even noticed how he interacted at his job in the drug store with a woman who had two little girls. He paid special attention to her children, and I thought then that he would be a good father. I answered him, "Yes," because as far as I knew, I did love him.

I told Mama he wanted to marry me before he left for France, so she talked to the preacher and our wedding ceremony was in the Pastor's living room and we had punch and wedding cake and took some pictures. We had to have our wedding quickly because he only had a short leave before he had to report back to the army base. So, we got married in the pastor's home with just our families in attendance, and then had our reception at his parents' house. After our wedding Daddy drove us to downtown Roanoke and dropped us off in front of our hotel. I felt like a Princess!

My farm life didn't prepare me for all the new things I would see and do for the next two years. In my naivete, when we got to the hotel room, I asked if we could eat and go dancing. I had no idea at all of what a man's thoughts would be on his wedding night. I was still a child in so many ways! So, we walked down the streets of Roanoke. I don't remember where or what we ate, but we took a taxi to a dance hall and danced and enjoyed just being there. I had never been to a dance hall before, so it was an exciting experience to be part of a party scene I had only seen in movies. In fact, the whole thing seemed unreal to me.

Back at the hotel, of course, it was bedtime. I guess there will be some readers that will find it hard to believe that I could have been so innocent—but innocent, I was! He was patient and kind and explained things to me. He never said anything negative, but I'm sure he was shocked at my lack of knowledge, not just the fact that I was a virgin. And I am thankful he was patient. We were there for one or two more nights, and that was our honeymoon. Daddy and my brother picked us up, drove us to the army base where we hugged goodbye, and the U.S. Army took him away to be with his unit stationed near Angoulême, France.

I kept busy with my grocery checker job at Kroger. When my older sister left her Kroger warehouse office job to be a lawyer's secretary, I was moved into her position. The only contact I had with my new husband was through the letters we wrote back and forth. We wrote letters for two months and then I received a government letter stating that the army would send me to France, and I was to have shots, obtain a passport and be at the army base on a particular date to be flown in an army airplane to Paris, France! I didn't know it was going to be such a short time before I would be following him. Getting everything done to pack away my childhood life and prepare for a two-year duty assignment in France with my Army PFC husband was exciting and scary!

Mama and Daddy and my little sister made the trip to the army base, where I would spend one night and then be put on an army plane with two propellers to fly across that huge Atlantic Ocean that I had never seen. I met other young wives on that trip. Mama actually kissed me on the cheek and Daddy gave me a really big hug. It was the first time I experienced either of those two things. My Mama's and Daddy's own childhood lives, I'm sure, did not have any outward show of affection. My Mother was orphaned as a young girl; and Daddy's parents were very busy, straight-laced, hard-working, farm people and showing emotions was not something they did.

I had never been away from home except for sleep-overs with high school girlfriends, or cousins; had never been on an airplane; and had never even seen the ocean until I was flying over it, looking down at tiny ships on a huge amount of water. Yes, I thought about the plane crashing and all that water and death; but even at eighteen, I had a strong faith in God, so I wasn't frightened. It was a big adventure, and I was looking forward to married life with my husband, being his wife, and all the possibilities of the future.

It was a long flight. When the plane landed, there was a huge crowd of people and soldiers, but I had no trouble finding my husband because at that time 6'2" people were not as plentiful as now. He broke through the lines and had his arms around me when an MP officer took him by the arm and put him back behind the ropes while I went through the "entrance procedure". It was an exhilarating time! I was excited to see my husband again and realized that I did love him and felt safe with him making decisions for us. I was never afraid. He easily spoke French to the French on the train, in restaurants, and everywhere we went. We had two or three days to sight-see in Paris before our train would leave for Angoulême in Southern France.

I knew nothing about France, so when we were climbing up a huge metal structure, I asked, "What is this thing?" and he said, "It's The Eiffel Tower!" My next question seemed to make a lot of sense to me, so I said, "What is The Eiffel Tower?" I got a history lesson there, at the Bastille (the Bastille Saint-Antoine), at the Arc de Triomphe, and several other places. I already knew about Notre-Dame (Cathédral Notre-Dame de Paris), Sacré-Cœur Basilica, and the huge museum—the Louvre—where the *Mona Lisa* hung openly, without armed guards. We ate Parisian food and drank coffee at an outdoor café overlooking the Seine River. It was like a fairytale, and I was The Princess enjoying all the fascinating things about Paris. We even went to the Moulin Rouge, fed pigeons in the parks, walked around all the water-fountains with their statues, and practiced saying French words. I felt completely at ease with him and never doubted my decision to be his wife.

Personal Development
Sin-Repentance-Renewal-Revival!

I have been thinking and praying about this part of my story for a long time because it is so intensely personal. I asked myself the question: What is the most important thing you want to accomplish in your life? I looked at my abilities: I'm intelligent, but I don't have a college degree. I wanted to be a Mama more than I wanted to be anything else. When I was married at age eighteen, just a few months out of high school, I thought I was all grown up! Maybe all eighteen year olds feel that way. In actuality, I was very much still a child, and it took years for me to develop into womanhood. I'm not sure where this is going. I'm just writing as I feel the Lord's Holy Spirit directing me. I have to be completely honest about everything because once you write something down and it gets printed, it is a record for eternity—in writing itself, but also in the minds of every reader. So, I have to pray over every word, to know the thoughts and intents of my heart.

> *"For the word of God is quick, and powerful, and sharper than any twoedged sword, piercing even to the dividing asunder of soul and spirit, and of the joints and marrow, and is a discerner of the thoughts and intents of the heart."*
> —HEBREWS 4:12 KJV

Then verse 13 gets even more personal when we read:

> *"Neither is there any creature that is not manifest in his sight: but all things are naked and opened unto the eyes of him with whom we have to do."*
> —HEBREWS 4:13 KJV

These verses are softened somewhat when we read about the other attributes of God, Himself:

> *"He that loveth not knoweth not God; for God is love."*
> —I JOHN 4:8 KJV

and a beloved verse:

> *"For God so loved the world, that he gave his only begotten Son, that whosoever believeth in him should not perish, but have everlasting life."*
> —JOHN 3:16 KJV

God sent us JESUS, so we could live forever in Heaven!

I've had to ask God to forgive me for a long list of sins several times and start over again. Repentance and Re-dedication to God is a wonderful, cleansing process that restores hope in God and hope in yourself. In 1986, I already noted before, I re-dedicated my life to the Lord and have been on a steady trail upwards ever since. People looking on from outside wouldn't know or see what was going on in my heart. I'm sure that is one reason God said:

> *" 'Judge not, that ye be not judged. For with what judgment ye judge, ye shall be judged . . . ' "*
> —MATTHEW 7: 1–2 KJV

> *"Therefore thou art inexcusable, O man, whosoever thou art that judgest: for wherein thou judgest another, thou condemnest thyself; for thou that judgest doest the same things."*
> —ROMANS 2:1 KJV

> *(Father God, You must direct what I am to write: first, for Your Glory; second, for the salvation of the souls of other people who have sinned like I have; and equally important, is the fact that, in order for this book to reach into the hearts of all readers, the truth must be told!)*

Only Jesus Christ, Your Son, Father God, has lived a perfect life! The very reason You sent Your Perfect Son to die for the sins of the whole world is because nobody would be able to come into Your Perfect Heaven to live after death unless we have been perfect in our life on this earth. You already knew none of us were going to be able to live perfectly because your arch-enemy, Satan, is determined that everyone will break at least one of Your laws; therefore, not one of Your men or women created in Your image could come to Heaven, when their life ended on earth. Life on earth is a test to see how we will live and whether or not we will take Jesus, Your Son's, payment for our sin. The one reason for God's creation of a world full of people is because He wanted millions of children and each one, with different abilities and situations, had to be tested before they died to see if they would choose Satan or the Loving Creator God as the One they would obey. Since Father God already knew that all would fail the test at some point in their life, there had to be a way provided for them to be cleared of their breaking God's laws or forgiven completely. God's perfect plan was to use His own Perfect Son, Jesus, as the One and Only Sacrifice to pay for every person's sin (regardless of how many sins or how wicked they were). Each person must decide for themselves whom they would choose as their Master to obey. So, you may ask, what about all those people who never heard of Jesus or lived before He was even born. God answers that question Himself in His Holy Bible:

"For God's [holy] wrath and indignation are revealed from heaven against all ungodliness and unrighteousness of men, who in their wickedness repress and hinder the truth and make it inoperative. For that which is known about God is evident to them and made plain in their inner consciousness, because God [Himself] has shown it to them. For ever since the creation of the world His invisible nature and attributes, that is, His eternal power and divinity, have been made intelligible and clearly discernible in and through the things that have been made (His handiworks). So [men] are without excuse [altogether without any defense or justification],"
—ROMANS 1:18–20 AMPC

83

I knew God by the time I was four or five years old. I talked to Him one time before I had even begun first grade at school, before I could read or write, except maybe my name. I remember standing outside our basement door one starry night, staring up at the sky and I said: "God, how can You see me, when there are so many stars in the sky and so many people on this earth, and I am so little?" I don't remember any kind of answer. I just felt so loved by God. I also knew, before I started school, and before I could read, that there were grown-up people who didn't always talk nice or act nice, as I described it in my childish mind. I decided very young I was never going to talk about colored people the way they did and was never going to call anyone a N——. I knew that wasn't the right way to talk about any person. God lived in my heart at a very young age. I grew up with a special knowledge, that I feel sure came from God, about how to be nice, tell the truth, don't cheat, lie, or steal anything. A very strong desire grew in me from that time, to be kind to people, especially to people who were different. The only way I could have known all that was through God because I was taken to church from the time I was born. The very saddest thing about my childhood is that my mother always thought I was bad and whipped me often, and I seldom even knew why. I knew early not to break the rules. I didn't want to break any rules. I wanted to be good. There was some kind of misconception about me that I never understood; so, I just accepted my lot in life, forgiving my mother, feeling sorry for her because her mother died when she was small, and her daddy died when she was fifteen years old. She was moved from kin to kin (I think) and ended up in Charleston, WV, at a wealthy couple's house and became a caretaker of a special needs child who was a "baby" until he died.

This is the first time in my life I have shared these very personal experiences and thoughts about my childhood, and the development of characteristics that would define who I am. (Thank You, Father, for helping me write this, as I am very aware that I sat not knowing what to write next, and Your voice spoke to my heart. I'm always amazed when that happens!)

I never undressed in front of anyone—not my mother or sisters or girls I spent the night with or cousins whose homes I stayed in overnight sometimes. No-one ever touched my body, except for light hugs on various occasions, except my future husband, and we never touched below the waist. I was so modest that I went to great lengths during gym class in high school to wash behind a shower curtain and even change clothes. I never listened to jokes or boy-talk or participated in girl-talk about personal things that would have embarrassed me.

When I was in my 50's, I worked with some men whom I had instructed from my first day of employment not to tell dirty jokes or use dirty language around me. I said: "If you do, you're going to hear a sermon about Jesus!" None of them did, until one day only one man was in the office. He came up to my desk and started talking. I thought he was just telling me a story about himself and his wife until he got to the end, and it was a very dirty joke. I certainly didn't laugh, just said firmly: "I told you not to ever tell me "dirty jokes". He got very angry and called me a "prude" and walked away. I wish I had said: "Thank you!" I'm telling this story to emphasize that I tried hard to keep my mind clean.

Another time, I was at a friend's house and was going to take a shower. When I reached in the linen closet for a towel, there were pornography pictures in between the towels! I actually had a difficult time overcoming the shock and almost instant Satanic appeal to keep looking! I was so surprised at my own reactions that I had to pray very hard for some time to recover and overcome that instant appeal. Porn is an addiction that takes the power of God to break! I never thought I would ever be in the position of having to fight against that, since my whole life I had tried to keep my mind clean. My own experience has helped me realize how strong addictions can be to anything! I firmly believe that all addictions can be broken by the power of God and only by the power of God. Addictions are a tool of Satan, and he is determined to destroy every person— especially Christians. I was determined Satan was not going to win, and he didn't! The power of God's Holy Spirit living inside me was stronger than the power of Satan and I was set free—never to do that again—and that was a long time ago!

While I am on the subject of addictions, I was addicted to cigarettes for a while. My husband gave me his cigarettes after we were married.

Then he ordered alcoholic drinks for me, which I had never tasted in my life. I didn't know how to not do what he said. This unveiling of my most personal self is going to be the most difficult part to write about; but with God's help, I will write it because I feel like a lot of people need to know how sin can get into your heart and how difficult it is to stop each sin after it becomes a habit. Satan used my childish innocence against me. Everyone needs to mature as they grow older. Perhaps there are a large number of people who will read this and discover that they had a similar experience. If anyone can learn how to break free from any particular sin because of my personal experience in breaking free, then *Praise God* for Him giving me the strength it takes to be completely honest about my own struggles and my Victory!

When I was still very young, I realized there was a big difference in the way my brother was treated, and the way we three girls were treated. I was never jealous of the special attention my brother got just because he was a boy. I figured out in my own mind that men were in charge of the home, men were in charge of businesses, men were in charge of keeping us safe in the police departments and the military, and men were in charge of running our government and deciding all the important things about our whole country. Even in medicine, men were the doctors and women were the nurses. Even at church, the men were in charge. They preached and taught men's classes, and women taught women and children and led the music. Women were schoolteachers and principals in schools until high school, when men were principals. My brother got his first car when he was, I think, sixteen years old. None of us three girls ever got a car. I loved my Daddy more than anybody! He was very hard-working, and I followed him everywhere when I was little, and even up to my early teens. I never disobeyed him, except one time, in the hayfield. Mama sent me to tell him supper was ready, and he said, "Go help your brother get the cows into the barnyard for milking." I said, "I'm hungry and Mama said supper's ready." Daddy gave me a pop on my bottom and said, "You do what I told you to do." He had never hit me before and it was a very light smack, but I was so shocked I ran, screaming and crying, to help my brother.

I tell this story to emphasize the fact that I was raised to see men in charge and to obey. That mind-set carried over in my marriage and all relationships with men. I didn't know how to even express a different opinion about anything, but just stayed quiet and let the men in my life be in charge. That was not a good thing. I grew up having no idea that I had rights as a person, or that I could express my own thoughts and feelings about anything at all. I am sure this sounds very strange to girls and women of today, but that was in the 40's and 50's, and so even as I aged in the 60's and 70's and 80's, I was pretty much controlled by the men in my life. I was gradually learning to speak up about some things; but as a general rule, I had a difficult time opening my mouth to disagree with a man about anything, and believe it or not, I was in my 50's before I began to understand the physical attraction between men and women. Needless to say (or maybe not) this vital lack of knowledge caused a great deal of trouble in my still-virgin-in-some-ways mind.

I am going to back up a bit—back to my life in France, remembering that I was an eighteen year old virgin, raised in rural Virginia, on a farm, in a Christian home, and knew absolutely nothing about the big, bad world. I thought all I had to do was keep on being me, telling the truth, doing the job of home-making, and my husband would do his part and we would have a good marriage and home-life while we traveled and saw the world and started our family and just enjoyed life. But—my husband was not a Christian and didn't want to attend the base church on Sunday, or read the Bible, or pray, or give the tithe, or live a Christian life. I stopped reading my Bible, also, and had never really learned how to pray, so it wasn't long before I was drawn in to his party lifestyle. He loved parties and fun with other people, so I was taken to the base club where there was music and drinking and loud talking, etc. Everyone I was around knew not to tell dirty jokes and to watch their language. I was a wet-blanket that "put out their fire". In other words, I was no fun to be around. I didn't know for a long time that I had married a compulsive gambler.

I'll make this short. I wanted a baby. So, after being in France for six months, I asked my husband if we could start our family. I got pregnant and our first baby girl was born after I had been in

France for fifteen months. I loved being a mother, but a baby just added stress to our marriage because of the change in activities, and financial restraints, and travel restrictions, and dealing with crying and sicknesses, and limited togetherness time. I was so naive; I had no idea that my husband wasn't as interested in having a family as I was. We seldom talked. A lot of nights he didn't come home. Friends said he had guard duty. I believed everything I was told because I told the truth, myself, and it never occurred to me that some people could lie, and it wouldn't bother them. My husband gave me my first alcoholic drink and I sipped it and was given cigarettes, but didn't much like that, so I didn't smoke until much later in life. My rosy picture of married life was smudged, but I loved my husband and just did whatever he said to do. Because of my belief in the man being in charge, it never occurred to me to argue or disagree with him.

The following is very difficult to write, but it is important, if anyone else is in the same type of situation. Truth or reality is so important if we are going to have good relationships with others, or, as in my situation, mature in a way that develops respect for myself, as well as for others.

While we lived in France, I found myself in the Army post doctor's office several times with infections I knew nothing about. They are now referred to as STDs. My lack of knowledge must have seemed ridiculous to the doctors, but they never asked any questions or made any statements about how I got infected. It took a long time for me to figure out what was going on. I never turned down my husband's sexual advances or made any accusations against him. In fact, we didn't discuss much of anything except things like where we were going on our trips, or about the baby's needs. I considered myself as being a pretty dull person to talk to and figured he needed more excitement or interests in life than I did. By the time we got back to the States, I felt pretty much like a failure in the area of conversation in relationships. I was still the under-educated farm girl.

My husband started college and found good jobs. He graduated from Roanoke College with a business degree by the time our family had added a son. We lived in Salem on thirteen acres of land, with a lot of woods and farmland all around, like the way I grew up. My husband bought a pony and a horse, and then, we had two ponies and I guess people looking in thought we had a great family life. The truth was that my husband was seldom home. He was a salesman and developed a love for golf and joined the country club and spent a lot of time away from home. I just continued with my mother role, which I loved doing. My children were everything to me, but I'm getting ahead of the basic story. I finally realized that my husband was having sex with other women that had diseases, and that was why I had infections. I didn't know the names or the symptoms. Sometimes I think he was trying to get me to just leave him and go back home, but I never would have done that. I was in a difficult situation and decided to just stick it out. The hardest part was that I felt so unloved. I didn't understand why he quit loving me. It wasn't until years later that I realized it was because he thought I was boring. We slept together, ate together, went places together, but we had no love connection.

When we came back to the U.S., I was two months pregnant with our second baby girl. Mama was just as mean to me as before, but when Daddy first saw me, he grabbed me and hugged me tight! He had never done that before! My in-laws had moved to Florida while we were gone, so we had no place to go when we first got home. There were plenty of empty beds in Mama and Daddy's house. My husband immediately found a job. We moved into a tiny shack next to my homeplace on our neighbor's farm. There were three usable rooms, one had the ceiling falling in. There was electricity, but that's all: no water, except a spring; no bathroom; no heat, except a wood stove. My husband talked to the V.A. and found out he could go to college free and buy a house with no down payment or very low down payment. He found a house between Roanoke and Salem for almost $5,000, so we bought it. We lived in the little shack only a few months. After our second daughter was born toward the end of July, he made me get a job at a fast-food restaurant and he put the girls in a nursery school. I did not want to work and leave my two little girls in that place for someone else to raise!

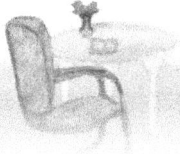

After France

The good times we had in France were the sight-seeing trips and the birth of our first child, a little girl. I had never wanted a career, and never thought about going to college because I knew Mama and Daddy didn't have the money. I never heard anything about student loans or scholarships either, so my future plans were what I had always dreamed about: getting married and being a mother.

During our two years in France, I began to realize how very different we were in our attitudes about life and marriage, and particularly about God. The lack of Christian values in his decision-making was one of our biggest problems. I stopped trying to attend church on the military base, stopped reading my Bible, and soon forgot to pray. I didn't learn in my church growing up that God uses the Words in His Book to answer our prayers, and since I wasn't reading it, and there was no one I could really talk to, I kept my broken heart to myself. However, I did talk to God about the problems that came up in my marriage.

So now we were back in the U.S.A. with an unknown future ahead of us. I was pregnant with our second child and had no thoughts or plans about working. I thought my place was at home—finding fulfillment in taking care of our children and the full-time job of homemaking. My husband started school on the G. I. Bill and went to work with no problem finding a job. He was gone a lot, but I understood that was how it had to be. The big problem in my heart was that I felt so unloved. I thought since we were back in the States, I would try to take the girls and go to church. I had no close friends and couldn't tell my family my problems. Everybody was busy with their own lives, so I held everything inside. For years I experienced hives all over my body, and it was a long time before I realized they were caused by my suppressed emotions. I tried several times to talk to my husband, but he had never learned how to really share his personal feelings, so we grew far apart. He went on with his life of college, studying, and working. He kept finding me jobs and insisting that I work, but as soon as he would get a better job or a raise, I would quit. I couldn't stand leaving my little girls in daycare.

My husband graduated with a business degree and found a sales job that required him to travel quite a lot. He made a very good salary, and we were able to take weekends away at the Greenbriar, the Homestead, and in Pinehurst, NC. We snow-skied and he played a lot of golf. It didn't bother him to leave our children; but I always missed them terribly, and two nights away was all I could stand at one time. My Daddy was our best babysitter! My kids loved him because he played games with them and was fun to be around. My big problem was that I felt so alone.

Our son was born after I specifically asked God to please let me have a boy (during our 7th year of marriage). What a joy it was and has been to have that prayer answered! My husband, intelligent and good-looking and having an out-going personality with others excelled at his job. However, at home, he just watched sports on TV, drank his beer, smoked his cigarettes, and demanded that the kids be quiet. Most of his free time was spent gambling on cards and sports games—I didn't even know that for years—and playing a lot of golf and partying at the country club. I hated country club life—but I played the good wife and dressed up in the kind of clothes he wanted me to wear, and had my hair styled every week at the salon (and kept it colored because it started turning grey early). I wore make-up, contact lenses, and false eyelashes, and I guess you could say I looked really good. Needless to say, our relationship was deteriorating.

Meanwhile, since my husband had graduated from college, I decided I could enroll in college. I began taking one course per year until I finally ended up with two years of college credits. I became a Certified Dental Assistant and worked five years as a Preventive Therapist. I had my own office and Therapy room and taught people how to take care of their teeth. I also had my own Dental room where I took X-rays, polished teeth, and assisted the doctor with patients who had TMJ (temporomandibular joint pain). In addition, I assisted with the creation of gold and porcelain crowns.

It was during this time that I developed a serious infection. My gynecologist insisted that I have a hysterectomy, so I did. While I was in the hospital for this surgery, I had an amazing experience with God that completely changed my life! I had been reading *The Cross and the Switchblade* by David Wilkerson and was touched by the power of The Holy Spirit on the gang members giving their hearts to Jesus. Also, around that same time, the dentist I worked for had taken me with his family to a prayer meeting at a Catholic church, where I was introduced to The Holy Spirit! He is God's Spirit, here on earth, living in the hearts of Christians who have truly been born again! When Jesus was here on earth, in the flesh of a man, He said:

"Nevertheless I tell you the truth; It is expedient for you that I go away: for if I go not away, the Comforter will not come unto you; but if I depart, I will send him unto you."
—JOHN 16:7 KJV

In the flesh, Jesus could be in only one place at a time—but The Holy Spirit can be in every Christian's heart at the same time! He's the One who gives us the ability to truly love one another and truly live the Christian life. We don't have any power of our own to live the Christian life. That is why so many Christians are still without power to overcome their sins, without power to witness, without power to have their prayers answered, and have no joy! I continued to worship in the Baptist church, but there is a significant difference in my worship and witness now that God's Holy Spirit is in me directing and empowering me!

Almost as soon as I recovered from that surgery, my husband left for good. I was thirty-six years old, and our children were fifteen, fourteen, and ten and a half. When he left, after eighteen years of marriage, I never had hives again. Not that life got a whole lot better, but that I was able to express my own feelings without having to always keep them pushed down inside. Even if reality was difficult or painful, I accepted the truth as being much better than pretending and became strong in all the areas I needed to be strong in as a divorced mother of three.

One of the things that helped me get over the end of my marriage was to forgive my ex-husband and forgive myself. This was not easy to do, but I wanted to be obedient, and I surely wanted my own sins forgiven. Jesus said:

> " 'For if you forgive men their trespasses, your heavenly Father will also forgive you. But if you do not forgive men their trespasses, neither will your Father forgive your trespasses.' "
> —MATTHEW 6:14–15 NKJV

The more we walk in obedience to the Word, the more we can expect Father God to bless us. I love Jesus, so I am going to try my best to obey Him.

> " 'He that hath my commandments, and keepeth them, he it is that loveth me: and he that loveth me shall be loved of my Father, and I will love him, and will manifest myself to him.' "
> —JOHN 14:21 KJV

> "Jesus answered and said to him, 'If anyone loves Me, he will keep My word; and My Father will love him, and We will come to him and make Our home with him. He who does not love Me does not keep My words; and the word which you hear is not Mine but the Father's who sent Me,' "
> —JOHN 14:23–24 NKJV

Money Money Money

No Money

When my husband first left, I had no idea he wasn't going to send any money at all! There was no money for the house payment, so for several months it just didn't get paid. I talked with the mortgage holder and, of course, my lawyer. We had two rental properties that also had mortgages. I had to use some of the rental money to pay other bills, so there were actually three mortgages that needed to be paid.

During that period of time, I got on my knees in front of the window that looked out over the thirteen acres we all loved and talked to my Heavenly Father. I had read about King Hezekiah in II Kings 19 when King Sennacherib of the Assyrians wrote a letter to King Hezekiah and told him he should not trust in his God to deliver him; that he had destroyed other nations and his God would not be able to save him, either. King Hezekiah took the letter into the temple and spread it out before the Lord, and asked the Lord to save him so all the kingdoms of the earth would know that He was The Lord God and there was no other god:

> *"And Hezekiah received the letter of the hand of the messengers, and read it: and Hezekiah went up into the house of the Lord, and spread it before the Lord. And Hezekiah prayed before the Lord, and said, O Lord God of Israel, which dwellest between the cherubims, thou art the God, even thou alone, of all the kingdoms of the earth; thou hast made heaven and earth. Lord, bow down thine ear, and hear: open, Lord, thine eyes, and see: and hear the words of Sennacherib, which hath sent him to*

reproach the living God. Of a truth, Lord, the kings of Assyria have destroyed the nations and their lands, . . . Now therefore, O Lord our God, I beseech thee, save thou us out of his hand, that all the kingdoms of the earth may know that thou art the Lord God, even thou only."

—II KINGS 19:14–17,19 KJV

I did just what King Hezekiah did. I spread all our bills out before the Lord and reminded Him that the land and the house where we lived belonged to Him and He was going to have to step in and direct me about what to do. And He did!

The Lord directed me to a Christian attorney, who not only arranged my divorce, but arranged for a realtor to sell the two rental properties. The divorce had a decree that I was to receive a certain amount of money each month for each child. I never received any money but refused to have my ex-husband arrested. The two rental properties sold, and all the back payments were paid off!

My oldest daughter turned sixteen and she got a job at a shoe factory. She didn't even tell me she was considering looking for a job! The year after that, her sister turned sixteen and she also got a job at the shoe factory. My son and I continued delivering the papers. Then I met a man who was also delivering newspapers. He was a Christian and we got along well together. We decided to marry, and my son wanted to deliver the paper route by himself. He was thirteen, so he was quite able to do that. I quit delivering papers because now there were two incomes.

The main thing I learned during that period of time was to let go and trust God. Trying to figure things out on my own led to stress and no answers; but when I prayed and waited patiently, just doing what was before me to do, God was working. Through the years I have learned that He really is The Perfect Father. His love for His children is shown in how He works things out for our good, if we love and obey Him. Romans 8:28 NKJV became a favorite verse of Scripture:

"And we know that all things work together for good to those who love God, to those who are the called according to His purpose."

— ROMANS 8:28 NKJV

Life went on. My three children worked their way through college. I'm so proud of them! At this point in my life, they have given me 10 beautiful, intelligent, talented grandchildren! Does that sound like a proud Grandma, or what? I also have five (now seven) of the absolute prettiest great-grandchildren in the world! Am I over-doing the praise? Well, if so, I guess I'm like all other grandparents!

Checks in the Mail

Many times I have prayed and had my needs met! At this moment, I recall three specific times when I prayed for money, I received a check in the mail! One was from my grandmother's inheritance. It had never occurred to me that she would leave me money when she died. Daddy died years before Grandma did, and I never thought about her having money to leave to her family. The second check was from a retirement fund I had at one of my jobs. I had forgotten all about it! A third time I prayed for money was years later. My house was very humid in the summer, and I couldn't afford air conditioning. The piano keys were sticking so badly the piano wouldn't even play. I asked the Lord about buying a dehumidifier. I said, "Lord, if you could let me know for sure whether to purchase this expensive machine, just for the pleasure I get from playing the piano, could You please give me half the cost? I can come up with the other half." The very next day I received a check in the mail! It was a dividend check from something I didn't even know paid dividends! And! It was for at least half, if not more, of the cost of the dehumidifier! I was so excited about my heavenly Father's love for me and His understanding of my desire to continue playing the piano!

God knows all the details of our life and He is such a loving Father. In the Bible, when John 21:25 NKJV says:

> *"And there are also many other things that Jesus did, which if they were written one by one, I suppose that even the world itself could not contain the books that would be written. Amen."*

This is so true. I could never write all the things Father God does for me! This is merely a collection of *some* of the examples of His marvelous love, provision, and care for me, Shirley, His daughter.

The Bible says:

". . . God Is Love."
—I John 4:8 NKJV

"For God so loved the world that He gave His only begotten Son, that whoever believes in Him should not perish but have everlasting life."
—JOHN 3:16 NKJV

He died a horrible death on the cross so that we might be saved—so we might be ABLE to share His love here on earth and to live forever with Him in Heaven.

"Jesus Christ is the same yesterday, today, and forever."
—HEBREWS 13:8 NKJV

And He will do the very same for you! He wants a real relationship with you. He knows you—all about you. But how well do you know Him? Ask Him to reveal Himself to you—now!

". . . Behold, now is the accepted time;
behold, now is the day of salvation."
—II CORINTHIANS 6:2 NKJV

Reality: Mid-Life Crisis

I f all this sounds like a too-good-to-be-true fairytale, let me throw in a little reality check! When I was in my mid-40s I had a classic mid-life crisis, and according to the dictionary and psychology books it is real. I have difficulty now believing it happened to me, but it did! The main lesson learned is that perfection doesn't happen on this earth, and we should never let our guard down, because Satan is a real enemy ready to pounce without warning—desiring to destroy everyone who is trying to live for Jesus. I Peter 5:8 says:

"Be sober, be vigilant; because your adversary the devil walks about like a roaring lion, seeking whom he may devour."

— I PETER 5:8 NKJV

The most difficult thing for me to deal with was knowing that when my son (the baby) graduated from college, he wasn't coming back to the Roanoke/Salem area to work. He had met a lot of young people from all over the U.S. He spent time sail-boating in Northern Virginia and going on camping trips across the country. After college, he learned fund-raising, knocking on doors, etc. with a group of environmentalists. He was so good-looking, fun, and intelligent, that he quickly rose to leadership. A long story made short, he had his sights set for things other than what our area seemed to offer.

My children don't even know this part of my story! The bottom literally dropped out of my life when I realized my son was gone, probably forever! So, I was in my 40s, a grandmother, my second marriage was deteriorating, and I had a classic mid-life breakdown along with my empty nest syndrome. I sold the property where I had raised my children and had such great memories, and I spent years trying to find my way back to the Lord and get meaning and direction for every day. I lived outside the Lord's will but was always struggling to get back the great peace and joy I once had. I rebelled against God, quit church, and led a sinful life for three and a half years.

I couldn't find my way back to God until I went with an unsaved friend to a little country church in Franklin County, Virginia, in 1986. The preacher said we should be living our lives in such a way that God, Himself, could examine us under a microscope and not find any sin! Of course, my heart was convicted, and I went down the aisle and rededicated myself to God. My friend accepted Jesus as Savior and was baptized the next week! He was fifty-seven years old and his praying mother (in her 80s) was so very excited to get to see him baptized before she died! I was so thankful to get my life back on track with the Lord! It has been an uphill battle since then; but, beginning in 1999 when I moved into my "Paradise," it has been a Glorious Victory! God just explained to me that the "Gift Card" was for me to use as proof that my recent sins were all paid for by Jesus. Every time I tell this story I am "redeeming my Gift Card" from God. Even after my three and a half years away from Him, the Lord made me feel so special. He gave me special attention with the Fortune and Paradise miracles, so no one could refute the truth of the fact that I am completely forgiven! I feel so blessed and so loved by God! He went to special extremes to make sure I knew I was forgiven. He has given me a whole new life since I moved into His house, joined the Baptist church, and went to work at the Christian counseling agency! I retired from there in 2008.

"Labeled"

Once a person has been "labeled" psychotic—whether it is true or not –it is almost impossible to change. However!

> *" '. . . with God all things are possible.' "*
> —MATTHEW 19:26 NKJV

I experienced an extremely traumatic incident over forty years ago when I was compelled to go to a psychiatric hospital by a cruel person, whose education and position of authority left me no option. I don't really want to go back and remember specific details because of the emotional trauma involved. I do know that without my strong Christian faith and the power of The Holy Spirit, I would not have been able to deal with the cruelty of the entire event.

I was employed as a receptionist, answering the phone for an entire office, typing letters, receiving visitors and packages, etc. I had to be able to do a lot of different things, meet a lot of people, remember names and details, and stay congenial all the time. One day, when everyone else was out of the office, I was physically attacked by an employee. I did not report the incident; mainly because I didn't want to cause a huge problem, but also because I didn't feel like I had any rights, and that it was something I just had to deal with myself. I didn't think anyone would believe me because the attacker was in management. Thank the Lord that the memory and all the details of that incident have been washed away by the Lord, as He healed me of this great trauma! The only thing I have to deal with now is other people's attitudes and their treatment of me as a psych patient. God heals all!

I do still have a clear memory of being an encouraging witness as a Christian to the other patients as well as the employees there.

I believe that God can take every negative event in our lives and use it to lift up the name of Jesus, as our Savior and King, and bring souls into the Kingdom of God! That was my attitude while I was living through the trauma and it is still my attitude! With the healing of the Spirit of God, I will continue to use the incident to hopefully bring more people into the family of God for healing of all kinds of hurt that people are dealing with.

I recently reread this account of the trauma I endured many years ago. My mental/psychological condition now is so calm, content, and full of the Joy of the Lord! I wish I could share my joy with the entire world! Maybe that is why the Lord has guided me to write about my life experiences, the good and the bad, to show what a wonderful, loving, healing God He is!

The only label I am looking forward to is: *Child of The Most High God!*

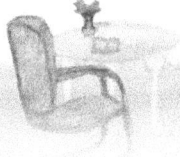

Spoiler Alert
Jail

I decided I was going to always tell the truth or not say anything at all. I didn't know some people thought lying was okay to do if it kept you out of trouble! My 3rd husband was a prime example of that. He was the biggest liar I ever saw. I met him through a "New Beginnings Group". They met in a church and got together for parties and picnics. Supposedly, everyone in the group was a Christian (who now found themselves divorced), and this group was considered to be "safe". Husband #3 was a small man with white hair, twinkling blue eyes and a big smile. He knew how to talk the Christian talk and wow the ladies. He came after me—big time—and I believed everything he said. So did my family. They even took his side after I divorced him. I've never met such a wicked man! I'm not going to write all the details because I don't want to relive the trauma I experienced! I found out later that he had been married and divorced many times. He stayed married just long enough to get his name on all the bank accounts and property he could, then set up an attack situation and have his wives arrested, while he ended up free with all their money. He tried it with me, but I had a good judge who saw through his lies; I came out scarred, but smarter, with my property and money.

I was profoundly traumatized because I did end up in jail overnight from his false accusations. I asked God how anything good could come out of that situation, because Romans 8:28 says that:

> *"And we know that all things work together for good to those who love God, to those who are the called according to His purpose."*
> — ROMANS 8:28 NKJV

103

He told me to do a jail ministry, so that is what I did for more than two and a half years. I recovered from the trauma and have good memories from the visits I made every Sunday to teach the Bible to the women in jail. Some were saved! I didn't know it at the time, but I was doing the same kind of thing Dr. Caroline Leaf teaches about in her book *Switch On Your Brain* about "changing a *toxic memory*". Upsetting memories bring bad emotions which can make us sick because they upset the normal functions of the body. God made us to be joyful and at peace about life, so Romans 8:28 gives us hope because we can trust God to make something good out of bad situations. Our job is to pray and ask Him to show us what good things we have learned or can learn from every bad experience. We must exercise our faith!

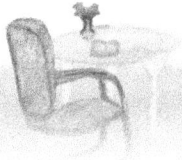

Back Pain
Healed

Another miracle has to do with my back. I had severe back pain for about sixty-five years due to an injury I suffered when I was a child. The doctor said another quarter inch and I would have been paralyzed. I stayed active continuously despite times of severe pain. However, as I got older, it became more and more difficult to even turn over in bed. One day, in particular, I thought I wouldn't be able to get up at all. I had been watching *The 700 Club with Pat Robertson* for years, and on this particular show I heard Pat say: "Someone born with scoliosis (curvature of the spine), has developed osteo-arthritis and stenosis in the spine." (Even though I wasn't born with scoliosis, I had the other symptoms.) I said out loud, "That's Me!" Pat said, "Stand up and put your hand on your lower back." So, I did what he said. He prayed for my healing. I waited a minute or two and didn't feel any different, but I said to myself, "I know how God does. I'll just wait and see." The next day, I went to my woodpile and was carrying an armload of wood to my porch, when I felt something like a weight lift off my lower back. I haven't had severe pain since.

Thank You, Jesus!

Un-Packing to Go Home

When we have been born again into the family of God, it also means we have died to our old life and our sinful nature, and we have been washed clean by Jesus with the power of His Word! That is just one reason for reading His written Word: The Holy Bible. As we read the Bible, God's Words of comfort and cleansing and hope make us new and clean from the contamination of the world! It is a verification and explanation of the phrase: *"Born Again!"*

I am filled with Joy, just writing my thoughts down, because I know God is speaking to me as I write! When I talk about "Un-packing" to go to Heaven, it is actually a process of letting go in our minds and hearts! We can't take anything negative into Heaven; there can be no hate or anger or frustration or negative thoughts of any kind! We have to un-pack and throw away any and all feelings and memories of the negative or hurtful parts of our lives! The mind and memory have to be healed, just as our bodies are completely healed as we enter the Presence of Jesus, our Lord, and the Almighty God of the Universe.

What kinds of things do I need to do before I leave this earth? What loose ends need to be tied? Are there apologies I need to make, forgiveness I need to ask for, forgive others for things they have done to me, or explanations I need to give for certain decisions? Do I need to choose who gets what of my possessions, or write down my preferences for my funeral? I need to be sure I have forgiven every person for any perceived wrongs done to me. Anything that causes me to have a little pause or catch in my spirit might be a sign that I need to clear my heart in that area. And, I need forgiveness, too.

When we leave this life, it is a joyful experience of looking forward to the beauty and purity of Heaven, and the inexplicable reality of the depth of the everlasting love and Presence of our Holy Father God! Jesus heals all! So we must spend time with Him, before we leave, and let Him heal everything that causes pain in our memory.

No baggage in Heaven!
Praise God!

Being in His Holy Presence
is our *FOREVER FORTUNE!*

and Being in Heaven
is our *FOREVER PARADISE!*

PRAISE GOD!

Author Bio

Shirley Morgan is a farm girl from Roanoke County, Virginia. She married a soldier, and while he was stationed in France, they traveled through Europe. In addition, she traveled on two mission trips to India. In the U.S., she has traveled all over the East Coast, from the Mississippi to the Atlantic and Maine to Florida. Now she is a Missionary at the Mill Mountain Star!

What began as a desperate plea to God about how to generate finances after a divorce, became an open door into God's heart—from which has poured out too-numerous-to-count answered prayers! Shirley was diagnosed with stage four breast cancer; hospice was called in—but God healed her! She needed a job, and God sent a woman by the last name of FORTUNE to help her. She needed a home, and God sent a woman by the last name of PARADIS to help her. She began visiting the Mill Mountain Star (which her uncle and cousins, the Kinseys, designed), and telling how God healed her to people from all over the world—one hundred and nineteen countries so far! She did many paintings in the 90s. God told her to put Scripture on some of her paintings and call them her *Memorial Paintings*. Shirley began giving them away, if interested, to visitors at the Star who had listened to her healing story. Her paintings with God's Word went back with those visitors all over the world.

Shirley is now eighty-five: a mother of three, a grandmother of ten and a great-grandmother of seven. At one time she was a foster mom. Her volunteer work has included: a jail ministry, Certified J&D Court Family Counselor, Certified for General District Court Mediation to receive referrals, a Notary Public, and nursing care for others. Shirley was employed thirty plus years in the workforce, which included: working as a Certified Dental Assistant & Prevention Therapist, retiring after ten years from General Electric, Receptionist for the Southwest Virginia U.S. Attorney's Office, Intake Assistant at a Christian counseling center, and various other office positions. For fun Shirley has enjoyed: writing, cooking, sewing, gardening, painting, homemaking, being a beautician for family and friends, doing "handyman" repairs, playing the piano (once, she learned how to play the banjo!), and of course reading her Bible—all the while talking to Father God. She wants to encourage you:

"If Father God can talk to a farm girl like me—every day—and answer my prayers about my life, my health and everything else, He can do the same for YOU!

As grateful as I am to be healed and walking in divine health, even more precious is knowing Jesus as my Savior, that He died for my sins, and I am able to tell others about Him, and have my paintings with His Word go all over the world."

—Shirley Morgan
"The Star Lady"

Life Verse:
"And my God shall supply all your need according to His riches in glory by Christ Jesus."
—PHILIPPIANS 4:19 NKJV

Resources & Interests

Throughout this story, the author mentions various resources and points of interest that were important to her story. She wanted to leave an easy reference list to encourage any reader that is interested in learning more.

The cover design is an original painting by the author, Shirley Morgan. To view more of her artwork, including some of her *Memorial Paintings*, please visit her website.

AUTHOR'S WEBSITE:
www.FortuneandParadise.com

BOOKS:
The Cross and The Switchblade by David Wilkerson
Operation World by Jason Mandryk
Pray for the World: A New Prayer Resource from Operation World
    Abridged from *Operation World 7th Edition* by Jason Mandryk
Radical by David Platt
Switch On Your Brain by Caroline Leaf

STUDY:
"*The Discovery Method*"
www.everyhome.org/bfam

FACILITIES:
Gentle Shepherd Hospice, Roanoke, VA
www.gentleshepherdhospice.com

RADIO/TV PROGRAMS:
The 700 Club
www.CBN.com The Christian Broadcasting Network
www1.cbn.com/700club

ATTRACTIONS:
"World's Largest Man-made Star" as the sign on Mill Mountain says.
www.playroanoke.com/the-roanoke-star/
www.visitroanokeva.com/things-to-do/attractions/roanoke-star/

PEOPLE:
Jane M. Fortune, LPC, LCMHC
www.carolinaforestcounseling.com

Special Thanks

```
      t          t          t
      h          h          h
      a          a          a
      n          n          n
        k          k          k
        y          y          y
        o          o          o
        u          u          u
```

"THANK YOU"

does NOT fully express my gratitude to my daughter,   A   N   K
Julie, for all her help in getting this work published.   H   Y
And, an extra special appreciation goes, of course, to   T   O
Megan Poling, COO and Director of Author Development,   U
Lucid Books, the entire Lucid team, and Clay Bridges Press   T
for all that make publishing, marketing, and a website happen.   H
A special thanks to Lisa for her ability to see what is important,   A
to coach, www.seedtimeharvestpublishing.com edit-edit-edit,   N
encourage, input, listen, reassure, keep boundaries, & market. K
Many thanks to Becky, Rebecca, SueAnn, Carole and Charlotte. Y U
And where would we be without all the prayers and warfare!   O
Fortune and Paradise could Not have been completed
without this great team that GOD put together!
Thank You to Bobby who quietly
endured the missing wife.
Especially, I Thank Father God for the gift of sharing His Love.
And I Thank you, Mother, for the privilege of helping you share
your love for Father God and His Love for you and all the world.